'Christianity in the UK in the 21st century has seen increasing numbers of Christian evangelists coming to the country in "reverse mission", helping to bring England back to the Gospel which it proclaimed centuries before and took to African nations. This cross-cultural communication is challenging and to have a book thinking through the implications of how such might be done, in the context of the postmodernity which is all too evident, is wonderful! Babatunde Adedibu has given us a thought-provoking, academically based, theologically sound and practical exposition of the importance of one key attribute as we share together – the power of storytelling. I hope every preacher in the country will read this book!'

Dr Peter Brierley
Lausanne Senior Associate for Research
Former Chief Executive Director
Christian Research, UK

'The book is certainly well researched and coming into the United Kingdom from another culture and background has added significance to the book. The personal encounters with British people and their complete bewilderment on being confronted with such concepts as "sin" and "repentance" is a shocking reminder of the sad point to which this once great Christian nation has come. How do we reach our generation for Christ? Are we "making sense" to people in a materialistic and "post Christian" culture? Are we preachers prepared to examine what we do and how we do it, or continue without change and claim we are being faithful in a day of small things? These issues are confronted and some thought provoking and challenging ideas put forward for the preacher's consideration in keeping or making the gospel sword sharp in these challenging and perilous times.'

Gregory Marshall
Pastor, Bible Pattern Church, Blackpool, UK

'This is a fascinating and insightful study on the role of storytelling in communicating the Christian Gospel. The author has skilfully researched the subject and offers pulpit communicators extremely useful material for reflection on the narrative technique as an essential tool in the task of proclamation and teaching biblical truth. I commend it to anyone seriously intent on sharing the gospel message with the uninitiated and uninformed.'

Rev Colin Warner
Former Acting Superintendent of Assemblies of God, UK
Professor of New Testament and Early Church,
Greenwich School of Theology, UK and
North West University, South Africa
(Potchefstroom Campus)

This is a book that needed writing.

Its author was born in Africa where there is a strong tradition of storytelling.

Coming to Britain where that tradition was not so deep seated and where the older familiarity, based on a knowledge of biblical stories has seen a serious decline, he challenges the present-day preacher to look seriously at the importance of storytelling to assist as a more effective means of communicating the truth of the unchanging Gospel in our post-modern society.

Taking a fresh look at the Gospels for example it is worth observing how these stories are told with their particular audiences in mind. Told well they catch the listener unawares. Most of these stories are very short; they are always to the point.

Many people today have a short retention for information; storytellers still write long novels that become bestsellers. With the greatest story in the world we could all tell it better. This book should help us to do that.

Desmond Cartwright, writer and official historian of
the Elim Pentecostal Church, UK

As I read Babatunde's book, I was reminded of my friend and fellow servant of the Lord, Reverend Lindsey Mann, who at our Mission Europe Conference segment of our Peniel 2008 said something which we found initially strange. He counselled that in our ('post-modern') society, 'one should not invite people to Church'. When you invite someone to church, the people's idea of Chuch is likely vastly different from mine. That person likely sees church as dull, boring and cold. So he will find it difficult to undertand why someone will invite him to such a place. But when you begin by telling him what great things we experince and enjoy in church such as the excitement, the uplifting danceable heavenly music, the relevant and life-transforming messages, the wonderful family and fellowship, then the invitee willbe eced and want to follow us to church. Babatunde's book shows us how to tell gospel through our life stories. I commend to everyone to read. Let's statrt telling stories!

Dr. Mark Osa Igiehon
Pastor RCCG Jesus House @ Aberdeen City of God

Storytelling:
An Effective Communication
Appeal in Preaching

A guide to reach the postmoderns

Babatunde Adedibu

First published in the United Kingdom in 2009
by Wisdom Summit

ISBN 978-0-9561800-0-1

Produced by
The Choir Press
www.thechoirpress.co.uk

All scripture quotations are taken from the King James Version of the Bible
unless indicated otherwise in the text.

Contents

Foreword

Writing in his groundbreaking bestseller, the author Oliver James commented on the Western world's obsession with consumerism in this way:

> To fill the emptiness and loneliness, and to replace our need for authentic, intimate relationships, we resort to the consumption that is essential for economic growth and profits. The more anxious or depressed we are, the more we must consume, and the more we consume, the more disturbed we become. Consumption holds out the false promise that our internal lack can be fixed by an external means.[1]

The Christian story which was deeply formative for much that has benefited Western culture, has now largely been replaced by the consumer story which in turn has led to a profound cultural crisis. Many in the Western world are deeply unhappy and in the view of many who are Christians, there is a need for a new evangelisation of the West.

Christians who have been brought up in the Western world are increasingly being joined in this task by those who have arrived in the West from parts of the world where the Christian Church is vital and flourishing. These new missionaries from other parts of the world (for that is what they are), do not find the task of reaching Western peoples

[1] Oliver James, *Affluenza*, Vermillion, 2007.

straightforward. Just as Western missionaries to Africa, South America and Asia had to learn in a previous generation how to communicate with the peoples and cultures that they encountered, so Christians arriving in the West face a similar and daunting challenge.

This imaginative book has been written by an African Christian who has risen to the task of seeking to reinterpret the faith he has grown up with in Africa so that the stories with which he is familiar might connect and transform the Westerners that he meets. In doing so he has come to see that culture and worldview must be taken seriously and that communication is vitally dependant on our ability to tell the ancient story of the Bible in ways that are comprehensible to a world of conspicuous consumption.

In penning these pages Babatunde has offered some priceless guideposts for others who would join him in the task. This is a thoughtful, perceptive and imaginative book and I commend it to all who have a passionate concern for the spiritual future of the Western world.

Dr Martin Robinson
Director
Together in Mission
Birmingham, UK

Preface
The Church in Transit

> 'Neither a wise man nor a brave man lies down on the
> tracks of history to wait for the train of the future to
> run over him.'
>
> Dwight David Eisenhower

The fluidity of culture and worldview in the last fifty years
in the West has ushered in a season of change in which we
are living witnesses of the demise of the world we had
known; and the values we have esteemed and lived for are
becoming alien to the emerging trends. The Church and the
communicators of the Gospel are thus inundated by
myriads of challenges, and the relevance of the Church is
often queried.

The paradigm shift from modernity to postmodernity
creates a dynamic tension for the Church and missionaries
in the West. This is because the operational modalities of
the modern era utilised by the Church and preachers cannot
be a vehicle for the transformation of the postmoderns as
ethos, knowledge and socio-cultural values of the two
eras are dissimilar. It is the story of new wine in a new skin
as the Church has to reinvent the wheel and respond
accordingly to challenges while at the same time not
compromising the integrity of the Word of God.

The Church is thus faced with a discontinuous change
that is quite dynamic and which has a multi-faceted impact
upon the values, lifestyles and spirituality of people. The

onerous challenge is basically how we can effectively communicate the Gospel in our communities where pluralism, relativism, consumerism, materialism and globalisation have shaped the values of people.

The Church today is coming to terms with the use of storytelling of the Gospel, returning to the founding days of the Gospel, when storytelling and parabolic sayings were a common feature in the ministry of Jesus, the preacher from the city of Galilee. It is quite intriguing to observe that there has been a renaissance of storytelling even in the business world in the twenty-first century, as various multi-national corporations are adopting storytelling to create corporate identity, values and vision.

Stories work best where the communicator understands the ethos, culture and worldview of the listeners while the process of proclamation becomes less difficult and better understood by the listener. Historically, storytelling was a major feature in Greco-Roman culture, and in Jewish culture, in which Jesus was referred to as a storyteller. Our understanding of Him rests on the various stories that we have heard about Him, which are called sermons.

There is a need for communicators to be realistic in view of the changes in the cultural climate and it is imperative whilst doing this to stay true to the Word by not removing the ancient landmarks of the Gospel. There exists the need for preachers to contextualise the Gospel in order to communicate effectively with the twenty-first-century listener as change and institutional values cannot be negotiated.

Babatunde Adedibu

Acknowledgements

The graciousness of God to me cannot be overemphasised as He has being the source of my inspiration and accomplishments. The foundation of my faith in Him was laid by the exemplary qualities and Christian virtues of James and Sarah Adedibu who nurtured me and my four brothers in the Fear of the Lord, Education and Diligence. I am eternally grateful to God for His faithfulness.

This book is the product of a generous friendship and mentoring relationship that I have enjoyed with Dr Martin Robinson which has shaped my life, character and deeper understanding of my potentials. I want to thank him for the wonderful privileges that I have shared with him and Lynda.

I am also grateful to the leadership of the Redeemed Christian Church of God under the amiable guidance of the General Overseer, Pastor E.A. Adeboye, which has nurtured me in the path of righteousness for almost two decades.

I am indebted to various congregations and theological institutions that I have worked with in Nigeria and the United Kingdom, which have served as sounding-boards for the various principles that are highlighted in this book. Your love, patience and appreciation of my potentials cannot be over emphasised.

The pathway to making this publication a reality was through the contributions of Prof Colin Warner, Dr

Richard Whitehouse, Dr Ajayi, Helen Ajimati, Tunji Omotade, Kola Arimoro and Harry Osemhanre who critiqued the manuscript at various stages.

In the words of Edwin Schlossberg, 'the skill of writing is to create a context in which other people can think', but this creative context has been made possible by Fiona Thornton, my editor, whose skills have turned my blurred strokes to an accessible literary piece. Miles Bailey and Action Publishing Technology for their effort to make this publication a reality. I would also like to express my gratitude to the staff of Blackpool library especially the local and family history section for their courteous services during the writing of the book.

Pastors Kola Bolanta, Jide Akinrinde (RIP), Adewunmi Oladunjoye, David-Sola Oludoyi and Bunmi Toyobo: your love and affection are unprecedented as enablers in my journey of faith. My appreciation to Pastors Yemi and Andrew Adeleke, Tayo and Yetunde Ayodele, Daniel Akhaemazea, Dupe Afolabi, Olujoke and Richard Odejayi, Olu Oyeusi, Omoyele Afolabi and others too numerous to mention for your contributions in my journey of faith in the United Kingdom.

Above all, I want to thank my childhood friend, lover and wife, Titilayo, for her deep love and affection for me over these years. You have indeed been a pillar of strength and encouragement as your understanding of my purpose has made this book a reality. There isn't a right word to describe the peace that your affection has given me over these years. Tobi and Toba, thanks for your patience with my not been there for as much as I would have loved to be, as you are not only God's gift to me as friends, brothers, admirers but fellow pilgrims in the journey of faith.

Jadesola

Introduction

'*One cannot help feeling the catastrophic drop in church attendance since the 1960s has been largely self induced by a fatal misreading of culture by the churches and theologians who supposedly service their needs.*'

Kieran Flanagan, as quoted by Michael Quicke

The submission of Kieran Flanagan paints a gloomy picture of the declining fortunes of the Church and the contributory factors to the present state of the Christian Church in the West. This looks more like indictment of the stakeholders of the Church, but are we to dismiss this submission without due consideration of the issues at stake? This might constitute 'treasonable felony' to preachers and theologians in the court of heaven! This is a clarion call to preachers and theologians to reflect contextually about the past, the present and what the future might be. Without adequate reflective practice into the reasons, the downward slide of the Christian faith in the West might be a difficult challenge to arrest: as communicators of eternal truth we need to render the good news relevant to the world we live in. The paradigm shift in the West has had tremendous impact on every facet of human existence and as such the Church, theologians and preachers cannot ignore the discontinuous cultural shift that has had and is still having reverberating effects within our social milieu.

The dramatic cultural shifts in the West of late have made previous cultural shifts seemingly insignificant. When Hurricane Katrina swept through New Orleans leaving trails of agony, pain and despair amongst the residents, the experience became a learning curve for adequate preparation for the arrival of hurricanes Gustav and Ike. Retrospection became an instrument to cope with future challenges of natural disaster: the United States government and her agencies failed in their previous response to minimise the devastating effect of Hurricane Katrina but were willing to confront and decapitate any hurricane threat in the future. What a model for the Church, theologians and preachers in terms of coping with fluidity and engagement of culture. Kieran Flanagan's assertion is a call to stakeholders of the Christian faith to adequately consider the various missiological and ecclesiological approaches to engage the dynamic worldviews of the twenty-first century listeners in order to communicate the Gospel effectively.

It seems most preachers and churches are still trapped within the confines of modernity and are perhaps out of reality with the prevailing worldview – postmodernity. It is indeed a statement of fact that our culture has undergone metamorphosis. The plight of such churches is illustrated by Robert Nash (1997: 18) as 'it [some churches] still swims in the fish bowl of modernity. Traditional churches advocate a carefully constructed and rational system of belief . . . Worship is well ordered, devoid of spontaneity . . . The focus of the church is on force feeding propositional truths about God to an American [Western] public that is crying out for an experience of God.' The Church of the twenty-first century in the West is confronted with a population that has a distinctive worldview that is antagonistic to the biblical worldview, that has its root in the effects of secularisation and pluralism which has resulted in the expulsion of God from the moral fibre of human composition, except for those who have held on to the 'old rugged cross'. It seems God is dead in our public life and has been interned in most private lives since six decades ago, and the memories many have was that there was once a God that ruled in the affairs of men!

The succinct implication is that the Church cannot continue to make use of the operational modalities of the modern era in a postmodern world. The message is still the same but the method must be reflective of the prevailing culture in order for effective communication to take place. Nash was quite economical in his choice of words as he constructively challenged the Church, preachers and theologians to understand the ethos of postmoderns. The prevailing condition of the postmodern is more experiential – not linear as it was during modernity – with visual, technological orientation and rabid resistance to structural authority and meta-narratives, but insatiable consumers. Haddon Robinson affirmed the change in his preaching style due to the cultural shift that had taken place over time; as he wrote in the preface to the second edition of his book *Biblical Preaching* (2001: 10), 'In the last twenty years, the culture has changed. Television and the computer have influenced the ways we learn and think. Narrative preaching has come into vogue ... I have spent a bit more time talking about narrative preaching this time around. Inductive sermons also reflect the influence of storied culture.'

This raises very fundamental questions with respect to the way preachers, and Bible study leaders, communicate God's message to people with a postmodern mindset. This is not limited to the un-churched, even the churched have been influenced greatly by the ethos of postmodernity; the only difference is the affirmation of the Lordship of Christ in their confession. It is pertinent to assert that the gospel message has not changed and will never change as such preachers must consistently engage the worldview of the listener to bring about effective communication while the Holy Spirit brings about the desired change in the life of the listeners. Graham Johnston (2002: 9) quoting William Willimon traced the genesis of the demise of the then known world: 'sometime between 1960 and 1980, an old world ended, and a fresh, new world began' that they say 'calls for renewed sense of what it means to be Christian and more precisely, of what it means to be pastors who care for Christians in a distinctly changed world'.

In the words of the Church of England, the Universal Church must have a 'fresh expression' in relation to the paradigm shift in every facet of church life, preaching inclusive. The inability of the twenty-first-century Church to cope with the dynamic cultural shift might stifle church life and have very precarious consequences for her. Leslie Newbigin, the British missiologist (1991: 12), noted the consequences of the isolationist disposition of the Church towards cultural shift and the Christian message as he referred to the Church as

> failing to understand and take seriously the world in which it is set, so that the gospel is not heard but remains incomprehensible because the church has sought security in its own past instead of risking its life in a deep involvement in the world. It can fail, on the other hand by allowing the world to dictate the issues and the terms of the meeting. The result then is that the world is not challenged at its depth but rather absorbs and domesticates the gospel and uses it to sacrilise its own purposes.

Cultural shift should not be a barrier to effective communication of the Gospel as the Word of God transcends culture, but preachers must be able to engage culture creatively and meaningfully with the postmodernist.

Preaching in the twenty-first century means preaching creatively in response to change. Preachers need to make preaching incarnational to postmoderns just as Jesus incarnated in order for the Word to become flesh. There has been massive shift in homiletical styles over various cultural shifts in the church life, from the traditional preaching style of communicating propositional truth, to kerygmatic preaching and the transformational preaching that was prevalent in the 1980s. Paul Wilson (1995: 12) captured the transitional phases of homiletical styles since the Middle Ages when he asserted that

> not since the Middle Ages or the reformation have such mighty winds swept the homiletical highlands. Theorists now speak of propositional and narrative; of deductive and inductive sermons; of different cultural understandings of preaching ... of the periscope and various criticism (historical, redaction, form, sociological, literary, canonical, rhetorical etc) of the role of the reader's experience; of changes in worship; of ways of thought being altered by mass media and computer technology.

There have been various views with respect to the effectiveness of the inductive and narrative preaching styles: though affirmed as being creative and imaginative, they might be grossly ineffective in biblical training and the theological depth that can sustain the growth, maturity and missional outlook of a Christian. It is quite important to realise that didactic preaching will still be relevant in the area of doctrinal training and preaching, but do not be surprised if it loses its pool of admirers – not as result of ineffectiveness, but relevance, as postmoderns are much more attracted and impacted by narrative preaching as it engages their worldview. The inability of preachers to engage with cultural shifts over time should not be unexpected, as in any change and adoption curve there will always be laggards that are not willing to get involved in new ways of doing things. However such preachers might have to contend with dwindling attendance, absence of dynamic youth membership and financial constraints.

My main purpose is to present a well articulated treatise for effective communication of the good news using storytelling to the postmodern generation. My attempt is not to open up a theological nor philosophical treatise on postmodernity but a synopsis of the salient features of the cultural shifts that can be used as leverage to communicate through storytelling the good news with postmoderns. I am persuaded that the complexities that have brought about the cultural shift in the West cannot be exhausted in a piece of writing but that much can be accomplished by preachers if they have very good understanding of the dynamics of the cultural trend and upholding the integrity of the Word of God. The starting point is to contextualise the method: as Leslie Newbigin (1991: 12) noted, 'I am trying to talk about the gospel – good news about something which happened and which in that sense does not change. The way of telling, it understanding it, however does change.'

Chapter 1

The Emerging Trends

The eerie rushing wind from the Atlantic Ocean greeted me with much gusto and unfriendliness as I stepped onto the soil of Blackpool in December 2006. Blackpool, a major tourist city in the United Kingdom, boasts all-year tourist attractions. The fierce winter gale was an immediate challenge in comparison to the cosmopolitan city of London I had left behind barely four hours earlier. The Promenade, a long stretch of road banked by the Atlantic Ocean on the right while entering into the city, is dotted with hotels with varying quality standards, bed and breakfast accommodation, pubs, bars, fish and chips shops and amusements centres. It is a well-lit street usually quite welcoming and amusing with all kinds of neon lights. It stretched my imagination and reminded me of my childhood story time of *Alice in Wonderland*.

On the seaside were a number of tourists admiring the beautiful scenery of the coastline; while some were trudging into cinemas, pubs, amusement centres and night clubs. Others were ecstatic with their Santa Claus caps on, enjoying the nightlife as they gratified their appetites as if pleasure was the end of life. Nightlife was not only spiced up by teenage lovebirds but the old and the young at heart, often trying to ignite old love flames and passion that age and the challenges of life might have quelled over the years.

'Welcome to the city of leisure and pleasure, this is certainly the Las Vegas of the United Kingdom,' was all I could hear in my spirit man. Various questions were rushing up and down in my brain as I looked through the window of the crawling cab that took me from the train station. The cab driver earnestly became my tour guide as it seemed he was enjoying every minute behind the wheel while the meter kept running. He was never tired of mentioning the names of pubs, the best night club and the best spots to hang out with a loved one. The cab stereo was a nuisance as the music that was being played did not make any sense to me. Intermittently he muttered some of the lyrics to himself and I was amused to learn that he was singing a genre of contemporary music referred to as 'garage'. I was confronted with the seemingly insurmountable challenge of how to communicate the Gospel to my host who obviously had a different worldview from the biblical worldview.

I asked him, 'Sir, do you know someone loves you?'

He smiled innocently and responded, 'Yes, Mum and Nicky love me.'

Indeed, he was quite right to know that not only one person loved him but he knew two people were there for him. I was jolted by his response, as my expectation was that he was going to ask me who the person was who loved him. The reality dawned on me that I was now confronted with the challenge of communicating with the cab driver about the saving grace of Jesus Christ.

I gathered my wits together and quickly responded, 'Nicky and your mum might love you but they cannot die for your sin.'

The cab driver was as quick to jump on my heels as a lion lying in wait for its prey; he looked shocked and responded with a barrage of questions. 'Why should they die for me? Their love for me doesn't have anything to do with dying for me. They like me, care for me and dote on me with gifts, affection, cuddles, kisses and we have memorable times together whenever I get to spend time with them. What do you mean by sin? Ain't got a clue about sin.' He stared at me through the inner mirror and asked again, 'Are you one of the religious folks?'

I responded, 'Yes, I'm a Christian.'

My response jolted my driver to reminisce about his early years. He said 'I went to church over thirty-five years ago when I was just eight years old because Victoria, my grandmother was a church folk and wouldn't allow you to stay with her except you attended church services with her on Sunday morning at one of the churches of Church of England at North Shore; I had little or no choice as my mum was a single mother who was having the best of times with her childhood sweetheart after she had me for my dad, who was not willing to be committed to her. I went for as long as I was compelled but after my ninth birthday I moved in with my mother and her partner, Paul. They were not church folks but were quite amiable, loving, fun-loving and party freaks. Paul was a chain smoker, man of many books and letters. He worked as an accounts officer with the City Council while mum worked as a nursery attendant in a primary school at North Shore.

'I grew up with Paul, mum and two younger sisters who were the product of the relationship with Paul. I hardly knew my dad who I met just twice during my teenage years. He was quite a nice guy, very reserved and quite ambitious. He said he was relocating to London to start a career in insurance brokerage. I took after him in appearance, voice and character and Mum would always chide me that I took after my dad.

'Life for us at that time was about doing well and I was never forced to make choices. I made my decisions based on my personal conviction. I remember Paul always telling us that, "Religion is the opium of the people." I guessed he got that from one of the numerous books he used to read. [This was a Karl Marx quote.] We were always fascinated and I'm still fascinated when people talk about life after death, that truth is absolute but you should know that truth is not absolute, as what you consider to be truth might not be truth to me. I am gay and have had a very steady partner for almost five years now. He is a very loving guy and I love him. We've been saving for our civil partnership ceremony next June, which we hope to consummate during the Glastonbury Festival. I have never loved a lady in my life and I have been gay for almost twenty years now. Men [*sic*] you got to explain what you mean by sin and those religious words to me.'

Our discourse came to an abrupt end as the cab driver pulled up in front of my destination but not without asking me a thought-provoking question: 'Why is it that, what most religious folks talk about God is very difficult to understand and irrelevant to many outside the Church?'

My cab driver's submission about the Church cannot be dismissed in entirety as Ken Costa, a Vice Chairman of UBS Investment Bank (one of the largest investment banks in the world) and chairman of Alpha International, in an interview with Agu Irukwu, the Executive Chairman of Mandate Men's Ministries based in the United Kingdom, in its maiden magazine (Winter 2007: 20), noted, 'the problem with the Church is that it is irrelevant to 95% of the people 95% of the time'. This calls for a rethink amongst church leaders. The words of Ken Costa are not just a sounding cymbal but a voice rich in wisdom and understanding of the challenges of the Christian faith in contemporary society and at the workplace which requires a paradigm shift in certain areas of church life.

The question posed not only lingered in my mind for quite some time but also aroused my curiosity on the challenges facing the Church in the Western world with regard to communication of the Gospel. The discourse between the cab driver and me is a reflection of the changes that have taken place in the Western world in the last fifty years as a result of the failure of the enlightenment age as values, taboos and morals have changed significantly.

Walter Truett Anderson (1995: 2) writes, 'We are in the midst of a great, confusing, stressful and enormously promising historical transition and it has to do with a change not so much in what we believe as in how we believe.' The operational modalities of some contemporary churches are still rooted in a culture and belief system produced by the enlightenment age but the stark realities in the Western world thrive on the ethos of postmodernity.

Current literature on the practice of missions in the Western world makes much comment on the shifts in praxis occasioned by the cultural shift, which is often characterised by the term postmodernity (Grenz 1996: 12). This shift is impacting upon thinking about the nature of Christian community, as well as worship, evangelism and mission.

The emerging culture is built around holism, connectedness to nature, aesthetics, emotion and intuition. Truth is relative and a deep-seated preference exists for relational authority. In comparison to modernity, the emerging culture of postmodernity subscribes to aesthetics, experiences, participation, image, connectivity and richness (Tomlinson 1995: 78; Sweet 2000: 111, 113).

This shift in cultural praxis is transitory and historically the Church has survived the transition from a pre-modern medieval worldview to the modern worldview. The response of the Church to these cultural shifts provides the answers to her survival. This response according to Leonard Sweet (2000) is referred to as 'Ancient Future Faith', which he describes as 'a faith that is both ancient and future, both historical and contemporary ... the Church [can] camp in the future in the light of the past'. The Church needs to actively engage in reflective thinking and active reorientation with respect to the lessons learnt from the past, the present and how to evolve in the future.

The historical antecedents of the transition of the Church are illustrated by the use of biblical narrative of God's engagement with Judah in the book of Jeremiah by Alan Roxburgh (2005: 72, 75). He observes that:

> massive discontinuous changes, on scales larger than we are currently experiencing, were always part of Israel's history. Our particular moment is part of the ongoing narrative of God's passionate, relentless encounters with those shaped by the biblical story ... In many ways; the today is in a

similar phase of transition Judah faced in Babylon. While this place is full of challenges and threats, it is also full of great opportunity for those who will seek to listen and understand.

The preacher is thus faced with a rare opportunity of communicating 'the good news' in this dynamic world of ours. The preacher is not at liberty to change the timeless riches committed into his hands by God but the manner by which he communicates Christ's riches to his listeners is not so rigid. The message ('What') is more important than the method of communication ('How') but the method must be effective. The method utilised in the delivery of a message can somewhat affect the effectiveness.

The Church is thus faced with a discontinuous change that is quite dynamic and which has a multi-faceted impact upon the values, lifestyles and spirituality of people. The onerous challenge is basically how we effectively communicate the Gospel in our communities where pluralism, relativism and globalisation have shaped the values of people. The aftermath of the cultural diversity is the emergence of divergent spiritualities: as such there exists the opinion amongst non-Christians that there are many pathways to God and you have diverse forms of spiritual expressions to choose from. For this reason Christianity cannot claim a monopoly of truth, as postmoderns do not believe in absolute truths, as truth is a product of what you make up by yourself. The biblical meta-narratives that were greatly affirmed prior to the enlightenment age have been replaced by the mini-narratives. Ethics and morals are a matter of choice as families encourage their children to make their own decisions on virtually everything in life. The fluidity of the prevailing cultural shift permeates every sphere of human endeavour. The basis of learning is no longer rational and logical but experiential. The Church is indeed in a post-Christian age. The discontinuous changes in culture have created enormous challenge to the Church as these changes seem obnoxious and force the Church to respond from all fronts. There is no doubt we live in an age where the only thing that we are sure of is change.

The Church is in one of the most challenging times ever as British theologian, Graham Ward (2000: 59, 60) noted: we live our lives based on experiential appeal, centred on consumerism, imagery and pluralism. He opines that:

> In this new city, the idea of distinct places is dispersed into a sea of universal placelesssness ... leading always to a single, human subject, the monadic consumer ... Community and social participation are telescoped into those shared emotional moments ... Cities are cities of the sign, concerned with image and culturally self conscious. In the post-modern city we have moved beyond individualism with a sense of communal feeling, to a new 'aesthetic paradigm' in which people come together in temporary emotional communities. These are regarded as fluid 'post-modern tribes' in which intense moments of ecstasy, empathy, and effectual immediacy are experienced.

The obvious question is what are the implications of this change to the community of believers and its missional implications to the communicators of the Gospel?

There are many implications of the obvious cultural shifts to the communicator of the Gospel, the Church and ministries. Richard Niebhur's (1951) writing on Christ and culture is a useful point of reference. He described five models of how the Church of Jesus Christ relates to culture: (1) Christ of culture, (2) Christ and culture paradox, (3) Christ above culture, (4) Christ against culture, and (5) Christ the transformer of culture (Niebhur 1951: vii). The Church needs a very firm understanding of the Christ and culture paradox in relation to its missional objectives.

The method of communication has to be dynamic as the cultural values have shifted and as such the communicative style must not be the same as that utilised during the modern era. For instance our culture is producing a different learning pattern. There has been shift from knowledge to experience, as the online issue of *Explorer* (March 2002) noted:

> Experience is the new currency of our culture. In the past we gained knowledge of a subject or issue and then later validated that knowledge. Today, people have an experience that is later validated by knowledge ... This shift has implications in the way we learn, communicate and interact. For Churches it impacts the design of worship, liturgy and the shape and content of the educational ministries, the process of spiritual formation and the design of sacred space and programming.

This negates the prevailing scenario in the modern Church that the purpose of preaching is the transmission of information to people. Due to the epistemology of modernism, communicating the Gospel is seen as speaking the truth. The weakness of this approach is that the timeless truth of the Gospel can become boring and simplistic as the listener's engagement to this propositional truth is only by assent. Brian Mclaren (cited in Bailey 1998 s6: 7) noted the contrast between stories and propositional statements during a conference on Perspectives Church, Gospel and Culture in the 21st Century. He said:

> Propositions come up and grab you by the lapels so that you can smell the coffee and cigarettes and Altoids on its breath. A story on the other hand sneaks up behind you, whispers in your ear, and when you turn around to see who's there, kicks you in the butt and goes and hides in the bushes.

This implies that story eliminates systemisation of truth and there is always an element of surprise in the unearthing of the moral of a story. Graham Johnston (2002: 149) addresses this neglect of listeners in *Preaching to a Postmodern World: A Guide to Reaching Twenty-first Century Listeners*:

Yet regard for the scripture, which is Strength, may also promote a weakness – a neglect of the listeners. Preachers may spend many hours poring over the text but little or no time considering the people who will receive the message. A key element to Jesus' preaching was the recognition and involvement of the listener.

The Church is presently in the age of participativeness. It is a common sight in the media that programmes are designed with the audience in mind to provide an avenue for participativeness. 'Who Wants to be a Millionaire?' a popular UK game show on ITV anchored by Chris Tarrant is a point of reference as the programme provides the audience with the opportunity to participate in the show through two out of the three lifelines during the game show. The 'Ask the Audience' lifeline gives the contestants the opportunity to ask the studio audience which answer they believe is correct. Members of the studio audience indicate their choice by selecting an answer. Or there is the 'Phone-a-friend' lifeline in which a contestant may call one of up to five pre-arranged friends. The design of the game, 'Who Wants to be a Millionaire?' is a reflection of postmodern ethos which is further espoused by the third lifeline, 'Fifty-fifty' in which the contestant asks the computer to eliminate two of the possible answer choices; the contestant is left with a choice of two answers, one of which is the correct answer. Engagement is a major feature of the show as the audience and friends of the contestants are involved in the programme. Another ethos of postmoderns evident in the programme is that the participants have an experience that is quite unique in its orientation in terms of the use of the neon lighting, music, fast-pace narration and use of suspense by Chris Tarrant to mesmerise not only the audience watching the programme but also the studio audience and the participants, thereby creating a community of viewers by connectedness.

The postmoderns are not to be blamed as the prevailing worldview – the only one that they know – defines their norms and belief system. Thus they are pluralistic, engage in spirituality and morality is oftentimes 'tossed' out of the window as issues of sexuality are not considered sacred but a matter of personal choice.

Gene Edward Veith (1995: 195) observed, 'Morality, like religion, is a matter of desire.' The ability of individuals to construct their own moral code is based on the principles of non-interference, which is a matter of personal desire. Personal desire and aspiration is foundational to postmodernists, as Veith (Ibid.) succinctly described the postmodern moral code:

> what I [postmoderns] want and choose is not only true but right (for me) ... that different people want and choose different things means that truth and morality are relative, but I have a right to my desires. Conversely, 'no one has the right' to criticise my desires and choices.

The Jeremy Kyle talk show on ITV1 is an amphitheatre from which to watch the postmodern debacle of moral wantonness. In one of the episodes, a teenager fiercely contested her friend's concerns about dating married men. Her friend insisted that it was morally wrong and that the relationship would take her nowhere. The young teenager tenaciously argued it is her right to define what she wants, and her desires are more important to her than a communal interpretation of her actions or concerns for her. The 'pick and mix' choices of the postmodernist have rendered taboos extinct: 'we live in a moral society – one in which "right" and "wrong" are categories with no universal meaning and everyone does what is right in his or her own eyes' (Robinson cited in Dobson 1993: 140). Morality is thus secondary to self for the postmodernist. This moral debacle is one of the numerous attitudes that the Church must confront with resolute determination as it is almost an endemic situation in the West and America.

Our communities, church inclusive, have witnessed and are witnessing decades of social decadence, aversion to morality, and utter contempt for self discipline leading to the 'death of God in Great Britain' using the words of Callum Brown. The level of moral perversion has not escaped the sight of politicians in our domain: many that are supposedly exemplary are themselves quite amoral as many politicians prefer moral neutrality in the spirit of political correctness. The leader of Conservative Party in Great Britain, David Cameron on 7th July 2008 at Glasgow could not but comment about the obvious moral decline in Great Britain as he acknowledged that: 'Bad. Good. Right. Wrong. These are words that our political system and our public sector scarcely dare use any more ... Refusing to use these words – right and wrong – means denial of personal responsibility and the concept of moral choice ...' It is quite amusing to realise that politicians are now acknowledging that the nation is on the precipice of moral chaos as society is already a demoralised society. David Cameron noted that complacency of the community is taking its toll on children in the community as he asserted, 'That is why our children are growing up without boundaries, thinking they can do as they please, and why no adult will intervene to stop them – including, often, their parents.' The observations of Cameron are not news to most British citizens as in the last ten years British teenagers have been identified with many social vices and classified worse than their European counterparts. The international edition of *Time* Magazine of 7th April 2008 describes the British youth scenario as, 'an epidemic of violent crime, teen pregnancy, and heavy drinking and drug abuse fuels fears that British youth is in Crisis.' Britain's moral decadence has reached its lowest ebb over the last decade. This has heralded a new phase in the troubled moral perverseness: the value of life and human dignity has been trivialised by youths as knife culture and gangsterism have skyrocketed, and teenagers kill with impunity, influenced by drugs, gang culture, family dysfunction and racial motivations. All this has heightened the already perverted moral chaos in United Kingdom. The statistics are appalling and a reflection of the 'death of God' in our public domain. According to a report published by the Prince's Trust that sampled almost two million (175,414) youths up to the age of 25years, 34% of the respondents do not have a parent whom they consider as a role model while 60% of the respondents are likely to turn to their peers during challenging periods as only 31% have the confidence to turn to their parents. This has eventually led to the emergence of defiant communities of youths whose values are shaped by the peculiarities of their challenges, thereby creating unique communities of role models within themselves that could have been found in the traditional communities – traditional communities that are fast fading away in our public life. The downward moral trend is not only a British problem but a Western challenge, as almost all countries in the West are on the downward moral slide.

The prevailing social decadence is not limited to moral challenges but a flagrant and irrepressible drug abuse in Europe. Britain is apparently miles ahead of other European countries in this debacle and has for five consecutive years topped the league table in Europe for drug abuse according to European Monitoring Centre for Drugs and Drug Addiction. The statistics are not only shocking but alarming and a reflection of the evil of our generation. According to the *Guardian* online (Guardian.co.uk) of November 6 2008, '12.7% of young adults aged 15 to 34 have used [cocaine].'

Indeed drug abuse is no respecter of class, race or gender: some in the British music industry perceive that snorting cocaine and opiates behind a music studio is synonymous with success! The obvious mistake is the fact that the public celebrate the gifts but are not so much interested in the character of the musicians who brazenly violate decency and above all truncate a promising career which might leave their families grieving. Drug abuse culture affects every segment of social life in Britain, even some members of the political class. It is in the light of the above that the Church of twenty-first-century Britain is confronted with monstrous social and moral challenges.

Barack Obama in his speech on 15 June 2008 to celebrate the annual Father's Day in America reiterated the
declining presence of male role models in families as he
posited that 'too many fathers are also missing – missing
from too many lives and too many homes. They have
abandoned their responsibilities, acting like boys instead
of men. And the foundations of our family have suffered
because of it ... we need fathers to realise that responsibility does not end at conception. We need them to realise
that what makes you a man is not the ability to have a
child – it's the courage to raise one.' Obama's assertion is
definitely from the experiential perspective as he grew to
accept the harsh realities of not having his dad in his life.
The American National Fatherhood Initiative's Father
Facts (www. Fatherhood.gov/statistics/index.cfm) gives a
more graphic picture of the absence of fathers in American
homes and the multiplier effects on the family unit, children and the communities. The facts are:

- 24 million children (34 percent) live absent their
  biological father.
- Nearly 20 million children (27 percent) live in single-
  parent homes.
- 1.35 million births (33 percent of all births) in 2000
  occurred out of wedlock.
- 43 percent of first marriages dissolve within fifteen
  years; about 60 percent of divorcing couples have children; and approximately one million children each
  year experience the divorce of their parents.
- Over 3.3 million children live with an unmarried
  parent and the parent's cohabiting partner.
- The number of cohabiting couples with children has
  nearly doubled since 1990, from 891,000 to 1.7
  million today.
- Fathers who live with their children are more likely to
  have a close, enduring relationship with their children
  than those who do not.
- The best predictor of father presence is marital status.

- Compared to children born within marriage, children born to cohabiting parents are three times as likely to experience father absence, and children born to unmarried, non-cohabiting parents are four times as likely to live in a father-absent home.
- About 40 percent of children in father-absent homes have not seen their father at all during the past year; 26 percent of absent fathers live in a different state than their children; and 50 percent of children living absent their father have never set foot in their father's home.
- Children who live absent their biological fathers are, on average, at least two to three times more likely to be poor, to use drugs, to experience educational, health, emotional and behavioral problems, to be victims of child abuse, and to engage in criminal behavior than their peers who live with their married, biological (or adoptive) parents.
- From 1960 to 1995, the proportion of children living in single-parent homes tripled, from 9 percent to 27 percent, and the proportion of children living with married parents declined.
- However, from 1995 to 2000, the proportion of children living in single-parent homes slightly declined, while the proportion of children living with two married parents remained stable.
- Children with involved, loving fathers are significantly more likely to do well in school, have healthy self-esteem, exhibit empathy and pro-social behavior, and avoid high-risk behaviors such as drug use, truancy, and criminal activity compared to children who have uninvolved fathers.
- Studies on parent-child relationships and child wellbeing show that father love is an important factor in predicting the social, emotional, and cognitive development and functioning of children and young adults

The moral onslaught is not a national crisis but a transatlantic phenomenon. Dr Jim Nelson Black, a cultural commentator, in his book *When Nations Die* examined the various empires that had risen and identified ten distinctive pathways towards their demise. Ironically, he noted that the United States is hanging on the cliff of spiritual and moral bankruptcy as he observed that the 'United States is at or near the top of all nations in the industrialised world in the rates of abortion, divorce and births to unwed mothers ... But in elementary and secondary education, we are at or near the bottom in achievement scores ... The spiritual and intellectual qualities of American life are seriously degraded and the soul of the nation is in jeopardy.' The gods of materialism, secularisation and pluralism are the tripartite hub of the Western world. British society is deeply materialistic, and that has been responsible for the churning out of people that are incredibly consumer oriented as most people's self-worth is defined by the measure of their wealth.

American television in the 1950s and 1960s is remembered for programmes such The adventures of Ozzie and Harriet, My Three Sons, Leave It To Beaver (1957–1963), The Munsters (1964–1966) and The Andy Griffith Show (1960–1968). These programmes were the epitome of traditional family values with very captivating storylines and they were in no way sexually explicit nor suggestive. By the 1970s and 1980s the trend was gradually reversed as soap operas such as *Dallas* and *Dynasty* became more prominent during prime time. These were successful but a complete departure from the 1950s as most of the programmes were at variance with traditional family values, showing total abhorrence of business ethics and dysfunctional family settings. The moral debacle seems to be progressive in the American TV industry with the advent of programmes such as *Sex and the City, Desperate Housewives* and the *Jerry Springer Show:* the word 'decency' is almost extinct in certain quarters in TV programming.

The American moral decline is summarised by a writer in the *Sunday Times Magazines* of 12th August 2007 before the commencement of the 2007 TV season, as it was observed that 'traditional appeals to family values find no resonance beyond the religious and conservative base. This has so emboldened America's TV executives, desperate to staunch the haemorrhaging of audiences to the internet, that the autumn schedules offers an orgy of sexually explicit programming – even [Janet] Jackson will be blushing.' The progressive moral decline of American TV production is a reflection of the signs of the times that the Church cannot shy away from. Indeed the West is suffering from 'Western World Moral and Religious Sclerosis Syndrome' (WWMRSS) – the failure of the West to confront moral and religious problems. There are ample pathological signs that the Western world needs to take heed of.

Communicators of the Gospel need to realise that unless we have initiatives to interact with the culture there will be an alienation of the harvest; and the harvest is really plenteous. The Church must face the obvious cultural realities of our times and must understand how to connect with the challenges through incarnational and ecclesiastical methods. The scope of Church's cultural assimilation should have a broad-spectrum appeal: the clarion call is for the Church to reinvent the wheel by utilising culturally relevant tools in the communication of the Gospel.

Effective communication of the Gospel to postmoderns requires that preachers retell God's story to the biblically illiterate generation. The prevailing cultural shift provides a learning curve for the Christian faith to cope with challenges of postmodernity. The preacher is thus invariably faced with the challenge of communicating with people who have no Judeo-Christian worldview as such. The communication of the Gospel as it was during the modern era which was firmly rooted in the Christian worldview needs no deconstruction as the preacher declares that the Bible says --- and people listen and respect the Word of God. But the storyline is no longer the same anymore as the claim to absolute truth by the Christian faith is challenged by postmoderns. They might ask what makes the Bible different from any other religious books in the bookshop. Colin S. Smith (2002: 74) in *Telling the Truth* noted:

> In the past ... preachers have been able to assume the basic building blocks of a Christian worldview ... You could take texts like John 3:16 or Romans 5:8 or Isaiah 53:4–6 and hang them on the clothesline of a Judeo-Christian world view. The problem in trying to reach postmodern people is that there is no clothesline ... the great challenge is to put up a clothesline.

This stems from the fact that postmodernists are very subjective in their views and as such they have relative opinions about issues. This means the contemporary preacher must have a deconstructionist approach by bringing into reality the story of God's grace to the teeming population of postmoderns by telling the story of God and humans.

Chapter 2

Understanding Times and Seasons

'We must all obey the law of change. It is the most powerful law of nature.'

Edmund Burke

The dynamic cultural shift in the last sixty years seems to be a geometric progression in the Western world and has reflected in diverse ways in the life of the Church. The Church must come to terms with the inescapable reality that cultural revolution takes its toll on the Church and as such the operational modalities of the Church in the nineteenth century in terms of music, leadership styles, communication, values and morals – cannot remain static and the Church must recognise that life in the twenty-first century is not the same. From the experiential perspective as an African in Diaspora this is more of a challenge to some African churches in United Kingdom as such churches' music, leadership and communication modalities are deeply rooted in the modern ethos. This implies that the cultural shift does not have any impact on the Church. The Church must understand that she cannot live in denial of the stark realities staring at her. There is an undeniable paradox that the Church needs to be much more aware of these realities as the ability or inability of the Church to interact with the culture can enhance or impair the missional objective of the Church. The boundary for the engagement of the culture by the Church is to repudiate any culture that is antagonistic to the Gospel rather than compromise its calling in the bid to engage culture.

Jesus engaged His audience within their cultural context and communicated the Gospel to them in indigenous form and was faithful to the scripture as He maintained the moral demands of the establishment of His kingdom motifs. In order to effectively communicate the good news to the populace through storytelling, the grounding conditions of the twenty-first century listeners must be understood. The understanding of the prevailing worldview – postmodernity and its associated features – will provide the basis for understanding the magnitude of its impact.

Church history is at a watershed with respect to the cultural shift from modernity to postmodernity. As such, it is impracticable not to 'speak of the Church without speaking of its mission, it [is] impossible to think of Church without thinking, in the same breadth, of [the Church] sent [into the world]' (Bosch 1991: 377).

Postmodernity has influenced great swathes of Europe and Western civilisation, and as such the understanding of the dynamics of postmodern culture will have far-reaching implications on leadership and missionary focus. Postmodernity is not merely the name of a new generation, but is rather a philosophical change that has taken place over time, and is the reaction against the preceding dispensation – modernity.

A critique of the core values of modernity could serve as the connecting point between the Church and the postmodern. In view of the missional objective of the Church, it is imperative that the leadership of the Church should reflect upon the cultural shift in order to discuss how culture and the Church should relate to each other: but the Church must never negotiate biblical truth in her attempt to be trans-cultural as the truth of the Gospel must never be abdicated while engaging the culture. In fact the Church must consistently challenge unacceptable cultural norms that contradict the Gospel.

In order to define the concepts of postmodernity and modernity, an overview of their respective worldviews is paramount. Friedrich Nietzsche's declaration of the 'death of God' marked a turning point in terms of the emergence or foreshadowing of a postmodern worldview. As James Sire (1997: 173) noted, 'The acknowledgment of the death of God is the beginning of postmodern wisdom.' Ironically, the emergence of postmodern wisdom seems to be the end of wisdom.

Sire (1997: 17) further elucidates on the concept of the worldview as 'a set of presuppositions (or assumptions) which we hold (consciously or unconsciously) about the basic make up of our world'. This view sums up the way that the belief systems of a population define the values and codes of conduct of its populace on virtually every issue of human endeavour. Walsh and Middleton (1984: 32) concur: 'a worldview provides a model of the world which guides its adherents in the world'. The basis of the actions and reactions of man is thus a reflection of the prevailing worldview that he or she subscribes to, as worldview shapes culture, norms and the values of society. Philips and Brown's (1991: 29) perspective has a broad-spectrum appeal by combining key features of Sire and Walsh and Middleton's definitions: 'worldview is first of all, an explanation and interpretation of the world and second an application of this view to life'.

Worldview provides an ontological and conceptual framework from which answers are arrived at. Walsh and Middleton (1984: 173) subscribe to this assertion, but noted that worldviews are quite different from philosophical systems: '[worldviews] are not to be confused with philosophical systems, although both are views of the totality of reality. Rather, worldviews are foundational to such systems ...' This implies that the basis of all philosophical systems is created by the prevailing worldview by which a populace chooses to understand the world and shape their ideas and beliefs.

There has been a rapid progression of various worldviews throughout history: for example the medieval world-view, which was Eurocentric, characterised by the teachings of the Church to create meaning in relation to the world and creation. During the modern era, meaning and signifi-cance are found through a search for facts, and the basis of reason is through objective observation and rational study. This is in direct comparison to postmodernism, which is cynical of meta-narratives and objectivity, believing instead that there is no absolute truth.

Sire (1997: 173) summarised the major cultural shifts and their peculiarities from premodern to postmodern thinking as follows:

> Movement from (1) a 'premodern' concern for a just society based on revelation from a just God to (2) a 'modern' attempt to use universal reason as the guide to justice to (3) a 'postmodern' despair of any universal standard for justice. Society then moves from medieval hierarchy to enlighten-ment democracy to post-modern anarchy.

The dynamics of the change of the various worldviews pres-ents an opportunity for an evaluation of the paradigm shift of society.

Gene Edward Veith (1995: 32–35) traced the historical emergence of modernity to the 1700s and observed that,

> the progress of science accelerated so rapidly that it seemed as if science could explain everything. This age of reason, scientific discovery, and human autonomy are termed the Enlightenment. Its thinkers embraced classicism with its order and rationality (although their version of classicism neglected the supernaturalism of Plato and Aristotle). However, they lumped Christianity together with paganism as outdated superstitions.

This depicts the mindset of the modernist: that enlighten-ment provides answers to man's search for the multitude of questions he is faced with. As Walsh and Middleton (1984: 11) summarised, 'The onset of postmodernity could be described as a loss of enthusiasm in the grounding conditions of modernity.'

Postmodernity

I am aware of the arguments amongst some sociologist like Anthony Giddens and Ulrich Beck who disagree with the idea of postmodernity but affirms the amergence of 'second modernity' as the alternative to postmodernity. The arguments about the cultural shift termed postmodernity or second modernity* is beyond the scope of this work but it is imperative to note that the two schools of thought agree that there has been a shift in the cultural trend from modernity. The scope of this book is to reflect on the cultural changes in the West and how to engage the new paradigm by Preachers in their homilies.

Many observers of postmodernity have commented that it is impossible to give a concise definition. This is further complicated by the fact that even noted authorities on postmodernity have to admit that the term 'postmodernism' is often applied to anything 'that the user of the term happens to like' (Hillborn, 1997: 6). Although it is true that there is no complete consensus on the meaning of the term, postmodernity is nevertheless a useful catch-all label to cover significant changes in the cultural landscape since the latter part of the twentieth century.

Postmodern has become a gregarious adjective, as it is associated with various wide-ranging terms, such as literature, art, philosophy, architecture, fiction, and cultural and literary criticism, amongst others. Postmodernity is a slippery concept. Mark Driscoll (2004: 161) noted that it is 'basically a philosophical junk drawer in which people toss anything and everything they cannot make sense of. If you ask four philoso-

---

* For detailed study of 'second modernity' or 'reflexive modernisation' see Krieken, R.V. Habibis. D. Smith, P. Hutchins, B. Haralambos, M. & M. Holborne. *Sociology: Themes and Perspectives (3rd Ed)*, Australia; Pearson Education, Australia. Giddens 2006, *Sociology (5th ed.)*, UK, Polity Press.

phers what postmodernity is, you will get five answers.'

Though scholars have divergent views of postmodernity, they uphold the view that the phenomenon marks the end of a single worldview philosophically. The emergence of postmodernity is the product of a loss of confidence in the grounding conditions of modernity. Consequently, almost all the core values of modernity are reversed and opposed. The brash confidence exhibited by exponents of modernity has given way to a more modest view of what can be achieved by the exercise of reason alone.

Grenz (1996: 12–13) noted the differences between Post-modernism, Postmodern and Postmodernity. He says Postmodernism *refers* to the

> intellectual mood and cultural expressions that are becom-ing increasingly dominant in contemporary society. These expressions call into question the ideals, principles, and values that lay at the heart of the modern mind-set. Post-modernity, in turn, refers to the era in which we are living; the time when the postmodern outlook increasingly shapes our society. The adjective postmodern, then, refers to the mind-set and its products ... Postmodernity is the era in which postmodern ideas, attitudes, and values reign – when the mood of postmodernism is moulding culture. This is the era of the postmodern society.

Postmodernism as a philosophical position may be anti-modern in its outlook (Grenz 1996: 12), but it would be too encompassing a judgement to say that this is true of postmodernity as a set of cultural experiences. Postmod-ernism mounts a number of telling criticisms of the modernist project; but while postmodern people share a critical stance towards modernism, ironically postmod-ernists utilise many of modernism's procedures and rely upon the fruits of its labour in their daily lives. Post-modernity accepts modernist rationality as a procedure in narrowly defined applications to technical problems, but places little confidence in it as a guiding life-principle. Postmodernism is, then, not so much anti-modern as the antithesis of modernity, as reflected in a number of areas of contemporary thought and practice.

A schematic typology of the antithesis between modernity and postmodernity was originally highlighted by Ihab Hassan, an Egyptian promoter of postmodern thought. A simplified version, adopted by Graham Johnston (2002: 27) is given below.

Table 1: Modernity vs. Postmodernity

Modernity	*Postmodernity*
Romantic view of life	Absurd view of life
Purpose	Play
Design	Chance
Hierarchy	Anarchy
A completed work	Process
Analysis from a distance	Analysis through participation
Creation/synthesis	Deconstruction/antithesis
Present	Absent
Centering	Dispersal
Semantics/words	Rhetoric/presentation
Depth	Surface
Narrative/*grande histoire*	Antinarrative/*petite histoire*
Metaphysics	Irony
Transcendence	Immanence

In his list Hassan (cited in Harvey 1990: 43) also includes the following, of particular relevance to this study:

God the Father	The Holy Ghost
Determinacy	Indeterminacy

The schema is made up of diverse fields ranging from theology to political science, linguistics, anthropology and philosophy, and sets a categorical opposition between modernity and postmodernity. Steven Connor (1989: 112) noted from the table that:

> Invisibly but unmistakably the mark of discredit hovers over the left-hand column, while the right-hand column, reads like

a list of all that is obviously desirable ... The effect of associating modernism with such drearily authoritarian principles as 'form', 'hierarchy', 'totalisation' and 'synthesis' is actually to deny the will-to-unmaking in modernism about which Hassan has had so much to say. Modernism now becomes the name for the purblind logo-centric past ... and Hassan is forced to rely on binary logic to promote the very things that appear to stand against binary logic, the ideas of dispersal, displacement and difference.

The obvious implication of the schema is that the values of the two eras are quite distinctive and almost antagonistic to each other. This thus gives insight into the values, norms and behavioural patterns of the two eras. The ability of the Church to understand the cultural context in which she is operating will contribute significantly to achieving its objectives.

McGrath (1994: 223) defined postmodernism as 'the pre-commitment to relativism or pluralism in relation to questions'. The problem, though, in understanding postmodernism is to define it beyond the perspectives of art, literature or architecture; but from an ideological perspective. It is a reactionary movement created at the collapse of modernity, which is best understood through a descriptive perspective.

James Sire (1997: 175) and Oden (cited in Veith, 1995: 24) characterised postmodernism as follows:

(a)   There has been a shift in 'first things' from being to knowing to constructing meaning.
(b)   The truth about reality is forever hidden from us. All we can do is tell stories [narratives].
(c)   All narratives mask a play for power. Any one narrative used as a meta-narrative is oppressive.
(d)   Human beings make themselves who they are by the languages they construct about themselves.
(e)   Ethics, like knowledge, is a linguistic construct. Social good is whatever society takes it to be.
(f)   The cutting edge of culture is literary theory.

According to Diogenes Allen (1989: 2), the transition from modernity to postmodernity is characterised by 'a massive intellectual revolution [which] is taking place that is perhaps as great as that which marked off the modern world from the Middle Ages. The foundations of the modern world are collapsing.'

Based on the work of the various scholars cited above, some of the key elements of postmodernism as a cultural phenomenon are:

(a) Subjectivity about absolute truth, as truth is defined by individuals and community.
(b) The 'death' of rationalism.
(c) Proliferation of choices.
(d) Individualism replaced by reawakening of interest in community.

While postmodernism rejects all meta-narratives and denies the validity of any worldview, it implicitly builds on its own worldview, albeit one that espouses pluralism, fragmentation and, ultimately, meaninglessness.

This cultural shift has practical consequences in terms of the way life is experienced in contemporary society. Practical implications arise from a postmodern perspective of the world, which directly impact upon planning decisions and modes of communication.

Due to the cultural shift from modernity to postmodernity, Stanley Grenz (1996:7) observed the effect of the change in the psyche of the emerging generation:

> members of the emerging generation are no longer confident that humanity will be able to solve the world's great problems or even that their economic situation will surpass that of their parents. They view life on earth as fragile and believe that the continued existence of mankind is dependent on a new attitude of cooperation rather than conquest.

Graham Johnston (2002: 26, 27) also sums up this perspective succinctly:

> So where modernity was cocky, postmodernity is anxious. Where modernity had all the answers, postmodernity is full of questions; where modernity clung to certainty and truth, postmodernity views the world as relative and subjective. Postmodern people have not only abandoned ideology and truth, but are likewise suspicious of those who claim to say, I know ... Postmodernity is the worldview that no worldview exists.

This is the bane of postmodern scepticism: postmodernists opine that truth is relative. A common feature of postmodernists is subscribing to the fact that each person or group of people has a different truth, which is only true within the context of the community that they belong to. Postmodernism is the rejection of a realist's understanding of knowledge and truth; a constructivist outlook that stands in opposition to modernity's objectivist stance.

The Condition of Postmodernity

The prevailing features of contemporary Western society have evolved under the influence of the market forces of late capitalism and postmodern theory. These factors are responsible for shaping the attitudes and behaviour of postmodern people in relation to the prevailing condition of postmodernity today. The most notable of these factors are as follows.

Cultural pluralism

Contemporary Western society is multicultural. But, as Newbigin (1989: 14) points out, 'cultures are not morally neutral, there are good and bad elements in any culture which must be judged on another basis'. A postmodern perspective of pluralism is quite different as it is based on the idea that a pluralistic society is inevitable since all knowledge is socially constructed and therefore anyone's claim to knowledge is as valid as anyone else's.

Modernity espoused two distinct realms of truth: the public truth, which is an arena of objective facts that may be arrived at by observation and which remain true for all people at all times, and private opinion, constituting values and beliefs that are not public. Invariably, public truth was thought to be monolithic and non-negotiable, but values and beliefs were held to be necessarily pluralistic because they were matters of personal interpretation rather than of fact.

This is antithetical to postmodern reasoning, which affirms that all knowledge is arrived at subjectively. Postmodern people therefore embrace a pluralistic society and are content to adopt many different versions of truth. Newbigin (1989: 224) describes postmodern society as a 'society where everything is subjective and relative, a society which has abandoned the belief that truth can be known and has settled for a purely subjective view of truth for you but not truth for all'.

The postmodern attitude to the transitory nature of truth is noted by Graham Cray (2000):

> The postmodern world has gone beyond an initial recognition of pluralism (the reality that there are competing truth claims) to relativism (that no truth can claim superiority over any other) and is now setting on constructivism (the claim that truth is something we construct to help us through life). The final postmodern move is thus from realism (the truth is out there to be found) to constructivism (we can make up truths to get by).

This observation depicts a worldview that is extremely dynamic, and as such the Church will need to take a multifaceted or holistic approach in communicating the Gospel to postmodern people.

Ian Banks (1997: 165) depicts the mindset of the postmodernist in his novel *A Song of Stone*, painting a bleak picture of agnostic Britain where disorder is prevalent.

Here the narrator eloquently expresses the ideology of the postmodern individual:

> We contain the universe inside ourselves, the totality of existence encompassed by all that we have to make sense of it; a grey ridged mushroom mass ladled into a bony bowl the size of a small cooking pot ... In more solipsistic moments I have conjectured that we do not simply experience everything within the squashed sphere, but created it there too. Perhaps we think up our own destinies and so in sense deserve whatever happens to us, for not having the wit to imagine something better.

This view is deconstructive, which negates objectivity and unchanging truths that God is the ultimate creator, as exemplified by the biblical perspective in the book of Genesis. Postmodern pluralism necessarily leads to further contemplation of the issues at hand.

The Western world, notably Britain and America, seems to have progressively become more pluralistic in the last fifty years. The Queen of Pop Music, Madonna, comments on her search for spirituality and epitomises the confusion most people in the Western world are facing due to the prevalence of pluralistic culture in the West. Madonna says, 'I go to synagogue, I study Hinduism, all paths lead to God.' Actress Halle Barry states, 'I believe in God. I just don't know if that God is Jehovah, Buddha or Allah' (cited in Kimball 2003: 67, 72). This constitutes a complex missionary challenge in the Western world as most of the population have been exposed to eclectic forms of spirituality and Christianity. Alan Walker (1957: 16) posited that 'the Western world is now the toughest mission field on earth. There is now more resistance to the Christian faith in the heart of old Christendom than anywhere else – England, Europe, Scandinavian, Canada, Austria and New Zealand. Only in United States is the church more than a minority movement'. But the church movement has become very dynamic in Africa, Latin America and Asia in the last three decades and these continents are now sending missionaries to the West. What a paradox – but could this be a case of the first becoming the last, or it is the season of harvest for the West as they are now benefiting from the seeds of evangelism sown in Asia and Africa?

The rise of pluralistic culture in America has been partly attributed to the effects of emigration to America: the United States has become the most religiously diverse nation in the world, since the Immigration Act of 1965 eliminated quotas linking immigration to national origins. Since then Muslims, Buddhists, Hindus, Sikhs, Jains, Zoroastrians and others have settled in the United States, radically altering the religious landscape. The obvious inference is that Christianity, which had hitherto been at the forefront as the normative source of spirituality, is now one of the numerous 'spirituality, lenses' acceptable in the West.

This view is valid but it might be argued by migrants that the degree of upsurge of pluralism in American society is far beyond emigration as most migrants would want to be respected for various contributions to the economy of the United States. This is a reflection of the obvious fact that emigration brings about the emergence of social and religious diversity globally. A similar trend is quite evident in the Britain of today: a more richly diverse society and culture compared with Britain of the Victorian age. This diversity is a reflection of multiple factors, which are historical in context, which include imperial invasion, economic emigration, forced migration due to famines, civil unrest and globalisation.

Relativism

Relativism is the aftermath of the acceptance of pluralism within postmodern society where truth is accepted on the basis of subjectivity. The modernist asks, 'What is true?' The postmodernist asks, 'What is truth for me?' This relativist approach often presents a major barrier in communicating the story of grace to postmoderns as it is not received objectively. The resultant effect is that people are left to make their own choice about what is true among competing versions of the truth, with no landmarks to guide them.

To the postmodern truth is up for grabs, as Robinson (1997: 31) noted:

> postmodernism says the ideas of a world are facts, or an objective truth is an illusion ... Everything is subjective. So the relative pluralism that was present in modernity (with regards to values and morality) has now extended to the whole of life. Everything is pluralistic now. All views are just as good as mine.

Johnston (2002: 30) illustrates the postmodern illusion through observation of the former American President Bill Clinton:

> When President Bill Clinton was asked in an interview about the compatibility of his Christian faith with his acceptance of homosexuality, he openly accepted the authority of the Bible, but disagreed that the Bible condemns homosexual practices as immoral ... it was his way of remaining true to the Bible while arguing that this is only an interpretative difference.

However, this is contrary to the biblical account from the perspective of Paul, who opined that homosexuality is not an interpretative issue, but an aberration to God (Romans 1:25–28). Clinton's point of view is a reflection of postmodern times: there is no universal truth, and truth is a matter of opinion.

The Christian faith no longer enjoys a privileged status in Britain as a Protestant nation by law. Pluralism has so infiltrated the very fibre of our existence that the issue of what is sacred is considered to be subjective. A point of reference was the comment of the Prince of Wales, Prince Charles, that he would prefer, as monarch, to be addressed as 'Defender of Faith' rather than 'Defender of the Faith'. This might seem to be an attempt to be politically correct due to pluralities of faith in Britain but what an irony: could such comments emanate from the custodian of Islamic faith in Saudi Arabia? Oh! Why are men bargaining the honour of God for men's commendation? This lends credence to the fact that in the postmodern world, to some Christianity is just one of the ways to worship God, and is a valid option but not the only way. This illustrates the fluidity of postmodernity as 'heavy-handed domination of modernity is replaced by the lightness of the postmodern carnival' (Newbigin 1989: 42). That faith is a matter of opinion and pluralities affords men the opportunity to 'pick and mix' to define their spiritual orientation as the Christian faith cannot claim monopoly of salvation. But this is a sharp departure from the Christian faith which maintains in no less but absolute terms that Jesus is the only pathway to salvation (Acts 4:12).

Social fragmentation

The cultural context of Western society is fragmented. Most postmoderns live inside a series of specialised compartments of activities that are quite distinct from work, home and leisure. Postmoderns reject meta-narratives that offer answers to the questions of life on epistemological and ethical grounds. Walsh and Middleton (1984: 70) vividly describe the mindset of postmodernists in this regard:

> If a narrative purports to be not simply a local story but the universal story of the world from *arche to teleos*, a grand narrative encompassing world history from beginning to end, then such a narrative inevitably claims more than it can possibly know ... But if metanarratives are social constructions, like abstract ethical systems, they are simply particular moral visions dressed up in the glue of universality ... The result is that all kind of events and people end up being excluded from the way in which the story gets told. No metanarrative, it appears, is large enough and open genuinely to include the experiences and realities of all people.

As a result, the ethical claim of postmoderns to justify the rejection of metanarratives is that they are 'inevitably oppressive and violent in their claims to "totality"' (Walsh and Middleton 1984: 71).

In the midst of social fragmentation, people seek connectedness. Postmoderns seek relationships that they construct for themselves as a result of this social fragmentation, rather than the kind of social interaction that was prevalent in the Enlightenment period. Sweet (2000: 113) observed that:

> Relationships stand at the heart of postmodern culture. As Apple Computers learned to its dismay, closed-system models are doomed to failure. Today it's all about relationships and partnerships ... the more digitally enhanced the culture becomes, the more flesh-and-blood the human enchantments. The more impersonal the transactions (economic, social, etc.), the deeper the hunger for relationships and community. Remote-control experiences of recordings sharpen and strengthen rather than eat away at communal experiences of live performances.

This is why postmoderns respond to relational authority rather than hierarchical authority. Relational authority is a matter of moral and pragmatic influence based on relationship rather than the exercise of naked power.

The Internet and mobile phone are examples of the desperation of postmodernists to be connected. Research conducted by tickbox.net on behalf of Lloyds TSB Bank in the United Kingdom in December 2004 showed the impact of technology on people in the United Kingdom. The condition has been dubbed Mobile and Internet Dependency Syndrome (MAIDS), and the research findings stated that:

> 63% of the respondents admitted they feel concerned if they leave their mobile phone at home and three quarters worried if they are unable to check their e-mails daily. When asked [what they had done when] they were half an hour away from home before realising they'd forgotten their

phone fifteen percent said they had made time to go back and collect while five percent said they become stressed when deprived of checking their inbox. Five per cent of respondents said they were seriously stressed if unable to check e-mails. (Lloyds TSB, 2005)

The driving force for this is not an obsession with technology, but to bring about a sense of connectedness, both emotionally and ontologically.

The fragmented self
The cultural shift from modernity to postmodernity contributes significantly to the collapse of an integrated worldview. The fragmented self built itself on the conception of the autonomous self, the idea that the individual as an independent observer of his or her world could arrive at knowledge of the truth about the external world by the exercise of reason, and thence go on to dominate and manipulate that world to his or her own advantage. Gibbs and Coffey (2000: 69) summed up the problem of the cultural shift:

> Now we are faced with a fragmented society characterized by confrontation as each piece strives to ensure its own survival and expand its power base. It is also a society of discontinuous change, which has rendered long-term strategic planning all but impossible. Targets move after you have fired the arrow, new targets pop up in unexpected places, and we are trying to aim from a lurching platform! This cultural chaos has affected all institutions.

This has led postmodernists to adopt numerous different personae, each persona socially constructed. As Walsh and Middleton (1984: 50) observed:

> Not only are many postmodern theorists insisting that the self is a construct or product of social systems, they are also making rather far-reaching claims about the role of discourse, or language, in this constitution of the self ... In

this postmodern appraisal, language is more a producer of subjectivity than a meaningful product of autonomous subjects.

Postmodernity grew out of the deconstruction movement, a major feature of which was the idea that meaning in language is not objectively understood and that interpretation is highly subjective. This has led to the problem of identity crisis among postmodernists as they have no anchor to view the world, and are unsure of their identity and how to relate to their world. Postmodern individuals are choked daily by the multiplicity of voices clamouring for their attention offering alternative identities.

Consumerism

Postmodernism has brought about the emergence of consumer capitalism, in which the prevalence of choice has rendered everything at par. Most Western consumers find themselves confronted by a sea of options and choices. Everything is relativised not so much by claims of the marginalised, but by the ability of postmodernists to choose anything from everything, ranging from opinions to goods and services. The 'consumer is king' philosophy has led to a lifestyle of self-gratification.

Henry Ford, the American car maker and industrialist, would never have imagined the magnitude of the impact of 'fordism' on the industrial, economic and political sectors, altering consumer behavioural patterns immeasurably beyond his days. Ford's rational approach to stimulating the consumer's desire was the genesis of the new technique of mass production, aesthetics and psychology. Harvey (1990: 125) summed up the impact of 'fordism':

> What was special about Ford ... was his vision, his explicit recognition that mass production means mass consumption, a new system of the reproduction of labour power, a new politics of labour control and management, a new aesthetics and psychology, in short, a new kind of rationalised, modernist and democratic society.

The story hasn't really changed since Ford's day, but has rather undergone a metamorphosis into customisation and personalisation. The production technique also changed the consumer behavioural pattern to mass customisation. For example, the Nike iD service allows consumers to customise a pair of boots or trainers. The customer can select from a wide range of colours, or give the size of their foot in millimetres and the name and number can be added to the boot tongue or heel.

The mass customisation of products is established in almost all manufacturing sectors. In the car industry, for example, at the Ford.co.uk website you can configure your dream car online, ranging from colour preference and interior leather to any other extra features that you might desire. The impact of global consumerism has even found its way to registration plate numbers, as some car owners are willing to pay more to have their plate customised. The key theme for most manufacturers is simply to offer whatever suits the customer's passing whim.

The 'information explosion' has brought about the stimulation of consumption through marketing techniques that rely upon the manipulation of images in order to promote products. The power of these marketing techniques cannot be overemphasised, as revealed by a marketing executive in a corporate training session on the PBS documentary *Affluenza*: 'you must get kids branded by age five if you want them as faithful consumers of your products' (cited in Sine 2003: 353). This depicts the marketing philosophy of the postmodernist, which is to brand children from a very tender age.

Postmodernists live in a world driven by image and technology. Often their perception is defined by what they consume, as postmodernists buy image and a sense of reassurance of their importance. This creates what is often referred to as 'retail therapy', as the goods they buy and consume are perceived to have value beyond the product.

The contemporary architectural designs of shopping malls have metamorphosed into temples, edifices of sacred space in which connectivity and meaning are established for the postmodern soul. The connectivity offers postmodernists an illusionary community as they seek to establish shared values and a personalised marketplace where relationships are created and celebrated. The catalyst for this is that most postmodern economic transactions are carried out through e-commerce. As Sweet (2000: 111) commented:

> More than buying and selling, the electronic emporium is about posting messages and maydays on bulletin boards, policing the integrity of transactions through the feedback forum, discovering new friends and launching new relationships at the eBay café. The Internet is becoming a key relational tool both for kids – as 51 per cent of teens to connect relationally with their peers – and for adults.

However, the magnitude of the connectivity brought about by the e-market is still an illusion as it cannot satisfy the deeper longings for significance in the community. Sweet (2000: 111) offered vivid insight into this phenomenon:

> The Internet is proving to be one of the greatest inventions in the history of civilisation. The primary arenas of social exchange and community engagement – workplace, shopping malls, and supermarkets – are being marginalised in a culture where sources of community are already hard to come by. The more connected we become electronically, the more disconnected we can become personally. One psychiatrist has a patient who calls her husband's computer 'his plastic mistress'.

The insatiable consumerism disposition of postmodernists creates massive opportunities for exploration by various manufacturers and service organisations to their advantage as huge profits are generated yearly through the World Wide Web. It would not be presumptuous to state that some websites have attained the status of a global phenomenon as they are consistently structured to align with the values of their customers.

EBay is perhaps one of the most visited sites on the World Wide Web for e-commerce as it consistently explores its understanding of the economic orientations and perceived ethos of its prospective customers. EBay is fast becoming institutionalised as it engages in various approaches of 'interactive relationship management': this might account for one who has traded on eBay always going back.

EBay brings about connectedness not only between the buyer and seller but also the story, image and the reputation of the seller as people bask in the euphoria of having an e-community. Facebook is also another growing phenomenon globally as not only does it connect people but it is also a veritable tool for e-commerce as well as social interaction. The social ties created by some of these e-commerce sites have tremendous impact upon most postmoderns as connectedness has been identified as having positive physical and emotional impact on people. The Church, in order to reduce the downslide in terms of membership and meeting the postmodern challenge, might need to examine her connectedness to people and the context of their connectedness.

Global culture, local identity

Postmodernity arose in the context of the cultural shift from manufacturing technology to information technology. The advent of radio marked the beginning of the shift of new means of cultural communication, later succeeded by television. Television and computers have more impact as media because radio does not require one's full attention. In contrast, televisions and computers pour out powerful images that command attention, and with these images come a wave of messages.

Murray (2004: 279) noted that the 'image colonialism' of people came with the advent of television:

> If there is any technological watershed of the postmodern, it lies here. If we compare the setting it has created to the opening of the [20th] century, the difference can be put quite simply. Once in jubilation or alarm, modernism was

seized by images of machinery; now postmodernism is sway to a machinery of images.

Information technology has become a central part of young people's lives, reflected in their worldview. However, ironically this often undermines the media, giving a false portrayal of lifestyles. As Steven Miles (2000: 72) argued, the media is 'full of portrayals that glamorise risky adult behaviour such as excessive drinking and sexual promiscuity'.

Lifestyles in the postmodern world are different from those in the past in terms of music, advertising, and fashion, and cultural icons are fast becoming models who define trends and opinions and provide seals of authentication on many advertisements. A very good example is Tissot, the popular watchmakers, who have recently produced a very limited brand of wristwatch branded 'Michael Owen', named after the English football player. The advertisement sends out the message that if it is good for Michael Owen, then it is good for everyone to have one. Evidently this influences the self-worth of postmodernists. The issue is not who you are, but what you identify with. Hence Hutchcraft (2000: 3–5) remarked, 'because they see it on television, in magazines, in advertisements, and everywhere they look, young people (in particular girls) think they have to be pretty, skinny, well-dressed and smart, otherwise they are not worth anything'. A typical example is the public outcry in Britain about size zero models' influence on the younger generation as many of the younger generation are seeking to do anything humanly possible to be a size zero. Many teenagers are fast losing their self-worth as they affirm that if you are not a size zero you are not a prospective model, nor indeed attractive or worthwhile as a person.

Information technology has gone a long way towards redefining public consciousness, creating a global technology conveying global images. This has led to the emergence of an eclectic globalised culture. This culture is predicated upon a dispersed means of production so that manufacturing and, increasingly, even service industries like insurance and telesales, are outsourced to the location of the cheapest labour forces and are marketed internationally.

For example, it has been a common occurrence in Britain in recent years for most service-orientated companies to relocate their call centres outside Britain. This tends to reduce labour overheads, as the cost of labour outside Britain is cheaper in comparison, and also creates employment in those countries. However, this tendency of globalisation has being seriously criticised as a process of exploitation of labour in the host countries, with the associated loss of job opportunities within the British economy (Behar 2003).

Postmodern people's economic demands are met via the global network as they buy goods that are designed, for instance, in England, manufactured in Japan, and supplied from anywhere in the global network. Ideas and images are consequently dispersed in much the same way. The global village is therefore a reality for most people today. Although our lives are still lived out locally, we are forced to think globally. The catchphrase for postmodern life has therefore become 'Think globally, act locally.'

Chapter 3

Story Time

'God made man because he loves stories.'
Rabbi Nachman of Bratzlev (as quoted
by Steve Sanfield)

'Story, story! Once upon a time, time! time!' This is a common introductory phrase that I grew up with in Africa while listening to stories at bedtime. It is a catchphrase that most storytellers utilise in introducing listeners to other worlds and our own world, which brings about connectedness of the listener and the storyteller. Storytelling is as natural to human beings as air is to the lungs as we (human beings) are creatures that think and act in response to stories as they touch our inner recess and convince us of truth. Every child grows up listening to stories whether you are an American listening to nursery rhymes or an African listening to fables or ancestral tales at moonlight in the village square. Listening to stories provides children with an unconscious opportunity to evaluate and accept established norms of a community which may influence their worldview for the rest of their lives.

The pertinent question is: are stories meant for children alone or can they be a tool in the hands of a preacher? Some critics are of the opinion that stories and illustrations have no place and little or no impact in preaching. They think that emphasis should primarily be focused on the historical and theological interpretation of the scripture. But this will absolutely negate the biblical model utilised by Jesus of Nazareth and the changes in the prevailing culture of contemporary times in which the twenty-first century listeners enjoy learning in a less linear fashion. From my experience in the ministry, most adults are more focused when listening to children's stories than sermons because stories have a way of putting us in touch with people, issues and challenges on a level of shared humanity.

Max DuPree (1989: 71, 72) noted the importance of storytelling in his book *Leadership is an Art*, describing a village experiencing electrification. He noted:

> Electricity had just been brought into the village where Dr Frost and his family were living. Each family got a single light in its hut. A real sign of progress. The trouble was that at night, though they had nothing to read and many of them did not know how to read, the families would sit in their huts in awe of this wonderful symbol of technology. The light-bulb watching began to replace the customary night time gatherings by the tribal fire, where the tribal story-tellers and elders would pass along the history of the tribe. The tribe was losing its history in the light of a few electric bulbs ... Every family, every college, every corporation, every institution needs tribal storytellers. The penalty for failing to listen is to lose one's historical context, one's binding values. Like the Nigerian tribe, without the continuity brought by custom, any group of people will begin to forget who they are.

Storytelling facilitated the transfer of historical and cultural values prior to the emergence of the print media but the importance of storytelling is still very much relevant beyond the oral tradition in sustaining man, history and cultural values.

Storytelling is an important part of human nature. It extends across generations and culture. Stories touch us emotionally and help fulfil our artistic and aesthetic desires. They are quite instructive about the world, history and major themes that affect man and his society. Storytelling is thus an interpersonal communication tool. Interpersonal communication is a powerful and universal tool among humans to interact with others. Social interaction breeds interconnectedness as it serves as the lifeline that nurtures and sustains the social milieu. Communication is of central importance to many aspects of human life as it is relational, purposeful and multidimensional. Forgas and Williams (2001: 7) noted,

> Homo sapiens is a highly sociable species ... Our impressive record of achievements owes a great deal to the highly elaborate strategies we have developed for getting along with each other and co-ordinating our interpersonal behaviours.

But there is a paradox; with the development of interpersonal communication man is still faced with the challenges of communicating effectively.

In the last two decades, there has been a renaissance in the art of storytelling and this seems to be predicated on the fact that many are continually seeking to engage their mind as a result of loneliness even from the religious perspective. William James offers an all time insight into the prevailing scenario of storytelling. He affirms that he 'believe[s] that feeling is deeper than the source of religion, and that philosophic and theological formulas are secondary products, like translations of a text into another tongue' (cited in Bausch 1984: 10). There exists the need for a stronger connection in the heart of man now than ever before: this need is inevitable in a world that is synonymous with change as the world is now a global village. The high-tech information age only brings about dissemination of information within the finger tips of mankind but it is devoid of connectedness as man is not engaging in face-to-face communication. Telecommunication, diverse home business and internet marketing have added to the gradual isolation of man, as the social milieu needed for continuous interaction is limited. As such, storytelling provides an avenue to engage the mind and permits the savouring of words.

This has brought about renewed interest in storytelling

not only in religious tales but in all sorts of tales. This is succinctly summed up by Rosemary Haughton (1973: 4) in *Tales From Eternity*: 'Fairy stories are never deliberately symbolic, yet they embody mankind's shrewdest and most realistic insights into human nature. We can use them to orientate ourselves in the present, and discover which way to go ...' Storytelling is a pathway to revisiting old issues from a different perspective as it helps people to understand and re-interpret creatively an unchangeable situation. This is due to the impact of stories on human emotion and reason. Preachers need to be cautious in the use of fairy stories as the truth value of some of the stories might be dubious and contradict the biblical teachings.

The perusal of the history of preaching from Jesus, Paul and New Testament perspectives vividly illustrates diversity of communicative styles of the New Testament Church. In the Gospels, Jesus is portrayed as a preacher, teacher and proclaimer. For instance in the Gospel according to Matthew: 'Then Jesus went about all the cities and villages, teaching in their synagogues, and proclaiming the good news of the kingdom' (Matthew 5:23) while the writer of the Gospel of Luke noted, 'He unrolled the scroll and found the place where it is written: "The Spirit of the Lord is upon me, because he has anointed me to bring good news to the poor"' (Luke 4:17–18). Mark describing the ministry of Jesus Christ in Galilee said, 'Now after John was arrested, Jesus came to Galilee proclaiming the good news of God' (Mark 1:14), 'When they found him, they said to him, "Everyone is searching for you.' He answered, 'Let us go on to the neighbouring towns, so that I may proclaim the message there also; for that is what I came to do"' (Mark 1:37–38).

The Greek words that describes Jesus' functionality as a preacher, proclaimer and teacher according to William Arndt and Wilbur Gingrich in *A Greek-English Lexicon of The New Testament* include *kerusso* 'to proclaim', *aggello* 'to announce', *euggalezio* 'to bring good news', *propheteuo* 'to prophesy', and *didasko* 'to teach'. However Sidney

Gredidamus observed that preaching has multiple usages in the New Testament. He noted that the New Testament 'uses as many as thirty-three different verbs to describe the single word preaching'. Paul was primarily a teacher (1 Cor 1:17). Paul's preaching was delivered in the context of Church worship services. Paul's preaching was 'primarily centred in conceptual argument, not narratives which dominate the Jesus tradition' (Wilson 1992: 25).

The various communicative functionalities of preaching, teaching and proclamation are differentiated by C. H. Dodd* (1937: 7, 8). He suggested that: 'Teaching (*didaskein*) is in a large majority of cases ethical instruction ... Preaching, on the other hand, is public proclamation of Christianity to a non-Christian world.' The post-resurrection ministry of the disciples was quite unique in comparison with Jesus' model of establishment of Kingdom truth through the use of stories and parables, but this might be attributable to the fact that the disciples' mandate was to demonstrate the proof of Christ's resurrection marked by signs and wonders to confound the sceptics. They were engaged in telling real-life stories enabled by their faith in Jesus (testimonies: Mk 16:15; Acts 4) but this does not prevent a preacher from contextual-ising the Gospel with the use of stories.

This distinction in the communicative styles of Jesus and Paul is quite important to preachers as almost sixty-five per cent of Christ's discourses in the Gospels were through storytelling and parables. The writer of the Gospel of Matthew noted that, 'All these things spake Jesus unto the multitude in parables, without which a parable spake he not unto them' (Matthew 13:34). Jesus engaged the multi-tude with the Kingdom of God using eight different parabolic sayings, after which He departed the Sea of Galilee to Nazareth His own country (verse 54). But in

* There have been various views expressed by contemporary scholars on Dodd's doctrinal views. For a detailed study see A. C. Thiselton's *Texts, Truth and Signification: Biblical Interpretation in The Modern Theologians: An Introduction to Christian Theology since 1918.* Eds David F. Ford and Rachel Muers, Blackwell Publishing, 2005.

verse eight of chapter thirteen after the first parable the multitude is clarified as 'those that are yet to come to the faith', like the seekers of truth in the postmodern era who are searching for 'spirituality'. The multitudes excluded the disciples: 'And the disciples came and said unto him, "Why speakest thou unto them [the multitudes] in parables?"' (verse 10). Jesus' response is quite instructive and revealing as He said unto them (the disciples), 'Because it is given unto you to know the mysteries of the kingdom of heaven but to them it is not given.' Jesus further substantiated His view when He said 'Therefore speak I to them in parables because they seeing see not; and hearing they hear not, neither do they understand' (Matthew 13:13). Dakes, in his commentary in *The Dake Annotated Reference Bible*, noted that the multitude were 'capable of understanding, but they refused to accept the truth, desiring to hold on to their old religious traditions and professions in preference to walking in the light of the truth'.

The height of the spiritual decadence of the multitude was depicted by the metaphor 'heart is waxed gross and their ears dull of hearing' which was referring to the multitudes to be converted. This cannot be viewed as failure of storytelling to bring about the conversion of the multitudes. The underlying truth is that storytelling cannot in itself bring about conversion – it aids the process of proclamation of the Gospel but every listener has a will to exercise in accepting the Gospel or rejecting it. In the above scenario Matthew used the metaphor to depict the degree of depravity of the minds of the multitude.

The disciples however, were given the mysteries of the kingdom of heaven which implies that they had accepted the revelation of the kingdom and as such the use of the parabolic sayings to the multitude, which was to make known new truths to interested hearers and seekers of truth and spirituality. The above scenario seems to support debate in homiletics on the distinction between *kerygma* and *diadche*. *Kerygma* is the proclamation or announcement of faith to those who do not yet believe, while *didache* is seen as something that follows *kerygma*. This line of thought has a positive correlation with Jesus' communication style as soon as He arrived in Galilee. The gospel according to Matthew (13:54) states that: 'And when he was come into his own country, he taught them in their synagogue, insomuch that they were astonished and said, whence this man this Wisdom, and these mighty works?'

The inherent tendency is to conclude that storytelling should be utilised in communicating the Gospel to those who are yet to come to the saving grace of Jesus Christ, but storytelling seems to have broad spectrum appeal in communication of the Gospel. This makes storytelling an evangelistic tool for all ages. This school of thought is supported by the famous British author of the Narnia series (which began in 1950 with the publication of *The Lion, the Witch and the Wardrobe*) and *Mere Christianity*, C.S. Lewis (1982: 73) who noted in 'Sometimes Fairy Stories May Say Best What's to be Said',

> I thought I saw how stories of this kind could steal past a certain inhibition which had paralyzed much of my own religion in childhood ... supposing that by casting all these things into an imaginary world, stripping them of their stained glass and Sunday school associations, one could make them for the first time appear in their real potency? Could one not thus steal past those watchful dragons? I thought one could.

This creates a lasting memory in the life of such listeners as most religious jargon is deliberately eliminated in storytelling the Gospel. Lewis was noted for his superb use of metaphor and in his work in Narnia, George Sayer his official biographer and friend noted that:

> His idea, as he once explained to me, was to make it easier for children to accept Christianity when they met it later in life. He hoped they would be vaguely reminded of the somewhat similar stories that they had read and enjoyed years before. 'I am aiming at a sort of pre-baptism of the child's imagination.'

The truth is that the Gospel might not be fully compre-
hended by children at their tender ages but the their
imagination would have been captured by Narnian images
of redemption: then when they listen to the Gospel, it will
resonate more readily through the power of imagery
utilised in the story of Narnia at the point of decision. This
might sound a little bit theoretical as there might not have
been substantive evidence from this postulation but Christian writers need to be cautious not to relegate the gospel
truth to 'fairytale' categories.

Chapter 4

Dynamics of Storytelling

Great leaders are noted for their ability to create connectedness with their audience through the art of storytelling. Evangelical scholars have also recognised that Jesus' emphasis on narrative offers a constructive model for communicating the Gospel in the twenty-first century. Jesus made extensive use of parables. In His discourses with His audience He spoke in ways that were relevant and stimulating by identifying with the needs of the people and bringing the audience to a level of divine consciousness through the use of parables and storylines.

His style was unique as His audiences were often left to make inference from His stories. David Norringhton (cited in Hillborn 1997: 154) gives this synopsis of His ministry:

> When we look at the ministry of Jesus in the Gospels, we see that he preached and taught substantially through the medium of parable and conversation. All in all, the sixty-odd parables and parabolic sayings represent about one-third of his recorded utterances. The majority of his other teaching was dialogical: it arose in debate with various experts in the Jewish law, in discussion with his disciples, and in the discourses he had with those he met on his travels. Sure enough, he made more formal didactic speeches from time to time, but these were infrequent by comparison.

Storytelling reveals life's meaning. Man is a natural storyteller who recounts experience, which recaptures humankind's oldest metaphor. Our journey as human beings has a beginning, middle and an end. These stories reconnect and live beyond the narrator.

Storytelling opens the door for metaphor to operate as stories often have a point beyond the mere surface line. They could be mythological and inherently imaginative, biblical stories inclusive. For instance, Jesus Christ's first miracle at the wedding at Cana, Galilee (John 2:1–12) was literally a demonstration of compassion on His part as the newly married couple were saved from social embarrassment on their wedding day. But there is more to it than meets the eye as there exists a lot of symbolism in the story. The occasion of the miracle was itself symbolic – a wedding feast is the symbol of the relationship of Jesus with the Church as He is the bridegroom and the Church represents His bride; while this relationship will be consummated at the marriage Supper of the Lamb. Barclays (cited in Bausch 1984: 115) subscribes to this perspective as he affirms that:

> We must always remember that beneath John's simple stories there is a deeper meaning which is open only to those who have eyes to see. In all his gospels John never writes any unnecessary or insignificant detail. Everything means something and everything points beyond.

It is, however, imperative to note that Bible scholars need to exercise restraint in the exegesis of biblical stories, to avoid isogesis which leads to heretical teachings.

America's political landscape has always being dotted by politicians who are astute storytellers. The likes of Abraham Lincoln, John F. Kennedy, Ronald Reagan, Bill Clinton, the maverick human rights activist Martin Luther King and the Democratic Party candidate in the 2008 United States of America presidential election, now the first African American President Barack Obama, communicate their political ideology through the use of storytelling. The Americans' dream of venturing to the moon was given impetus when President John F. Kennedy mobilised the nation on 12th September 1963 through the power of storytelling to 'put man on the moon' and return him safely to earth. Bill Clinton was quite emphatic about the influence of storytelling on his political orientation. He said: 'I grew up in the pre-television age, in a family of uneducated but smart, hard-working, caring storytellers. They taught me that everyone has a story. And that made politics intensely personal to me. It was about giving people better stories.' Bill Clinton makes other people part of his own narrative and this had tremendous impact on the populace as he identified with the challenges and the aspirations of the public in pursuit of the American dream. The ascendancy of Barack Obama to the White House was hewn out of his personal aspiration to fulfil the American dream for his life and generation one hundred and forty three years after Abraham Lincoln declared America an egalitarian country with the Emancipation proclamation of January 1, 1863. Most political analysts had identified him as charismatic, optimistic and persuasive in his pursuits, but above all he is a wonderful storyteller in the league of Ronald Reagan and Bill Clinton. His persuasive skill is borne out of a deep understanding and identifying with the stories of American citizens in pursuit of the American dream as he asserted that 'each day, it seems, thousands of Americans are going about their daily rounds – dropping off the kids at school, driving to the office, flying to a business meeting, shopping at the mall, trying to stay on their diets – and coming to the realization that something is missing. They are deciding that their work, their possessions, their diversions, their sheer busyness are not enough. They want a sense of purpose, a narrative arc to their lives, something that will relieve a chronic loneliness or lift them above the exhausting, relentless toil of daily life" (Barack Obama cited in Green and Robinson 2008: 113). It is quite intriguing that the political landscape of America is gradually churning out storytellers as presidents.

Barack Obama is a man who has a deep understanding of reconciling the challenges, pain, agony and the tribulations of the past in relation to the triumph of the present and a reassurance that the gains of the present provide insight to opportunities that the future holds for every American. He connected with the emotions of the African Americans as his election victory became a unifying factor amongst Americans – probably because his political ascendancy heralded the emergence of a new dawn in American politics. The climax was the consistency with which he made use of the many mini narratives of the experiences of others to conceptualise the end of the old order and the emergence of the new era in American politics. Jesse Jackson could not but weep – not so much for the joy of the success as a democrat, but more because of the narratives which were part of his life, the histories of others and the sacrifices of others. Obama said

> This election had many firsts and many stories that will be told for generations. But one that's on my mind tonight is about a woman who cast her ballot in Atlanta. She's a lot like the millions of others who stood in line to make their voice heard in this election except for one thing - Ann Nixon Cooper is 106 years old. She was born just a generation past slavery; a time when there were no cars on the road or planes in the sky; when someone like her couldn't vote for two reasons – because she was a woman and because of the color of her skin. And tonight, I think about all that she's seen throughout her century in America - the heartache and the hope; the struggle and the progress; the times we were told that we can't, and the people who pressed on with that American creed: Yes we can. At a time when women's voices were silenced and their hopes dismissed, she lived to see them stand up and speak out and reach for the ballot. Yes we can. When there was despair in the dust bowl and depression across the land, she saw a nation conquer fear itself with a New Deal, new jobs and a new sense of common purpose. Yes we can. When the bombs fell on our harbor and tyranny threatened the world, she was there to witness a generation rise to greatness and a democracy was saved. Yes we can. She was there for the buses in Montgomery, the hoses in Birmingham, a bridge in Selma, and a preacher from Atlanta who told a people that 'We Shall Overcome.' Yes we can. A man touched down on

the moon, a wall came down in Berlin, a world was connected by our own science and imagination. And this year, in this election, she touched her finger to a screen, and cast her vote, because after 106 years in America, through the best of times and the darkest of hours, she knows how America can change. Yes we can.

His words were not mere rhetoric but well structured historical mini narratives that evoke memories of the ugly, the bad and the good in American history. Such is the evocative power of storytelling: it has the ability to reminisce about the past while at same time celebrating present achievements.

There is no doubt that the 'destiny of the world is determined less by the battles that are lost and won than by the stories it loves and believes in' (Howard Goddard cited in Clark 2004: 12). Storytelling has also been a medium of transformation for many corporate organisations. Business leaders communicate their organisational values and vision to their employees, prospective recruits, customers and stockholders; as they create a corporate storyline by playing the same chord to bring about a symphony within the organisation and the enactment of those values as part of their daily responsibilities.

Organisational storytelling is a field which is generating interest in the business world. Strategic narratives are seen as a way for the organisation to express its internal values to both the internal staff and external public. Gordon Shaw et al. (1998) of 3M corroborated this, noting that:

> [Organisational story-telling is] central to our identity – part of the way we see ourselves and explain ourselves to one another. Stories are a habit of mind at 3M, and it's through them -through the way they make us see ourselves and our business operations in complex, multidimensional forms – that we're able to discover opportunities for strategic change. Stories give us ways to form ideas about winning.

Storytelling thus is a medium of transition to effect change. Major international financial institutions such as the World Bank and multinational corporations like Nike, IBM and South West Airlines have adopted storytelling as an effective tool of communication. One governmental organisation that has discovered the value of storytelling is the National Aeronautics and Space Agency (NASA) as Boyd (cited in Clark 2004: 193) observed that:

> The use of stories for knowledge sharing has been so effective at NASA ... we [NASA] also use stories to tell our employees the history of our firm so they can get a sense of our culture and get to know us more quickly. Our history helps them understand where we're going and of course, people enjoy seeing their stories in print.

In corporate storytelling the exchange occurs through the gamut of corporate communication media: advertising, press releases, corporate memos, sponsorships etc. Stories reveal what is unique about a company's aims and help a company's management, as a useful reminder that what matters most of all is focus.

Storytelling offers an organisation a way to communicate holistically with its public in a symbolic way. It offers meaning to corporate action in the environment as organisations exist only in so far as their members create them through discourse. Within this context, organisational stories become central to the way in which the organisation constructs meaning and makes sense of itself and its environment.

David Armstrong's revolutionary management approach greatly transformed his organisation as he had tried various management techniques including management by objectives, X Theory, one minute manager etc. But ever since he discovered the power of storytelling, Armstrong International has never been the same. Storytelling is now part of the organisational culture and he posits that:

> 'To keep our culture alive, I post stories on bulletin boards,

I put them in pay check envelopes and we've some to [hang] on the walls as decorations. We've recorded stories on CD to allow salespersons to listen in their cars and we've recorded several videotapes that we play on TV sets installed in the factories. A lot of people want to re-enact their own stories, and everybody enjoys watching a 3–4 minutes story. (Clarke 2004: 9)

This approach answers three pertinent questions indirectly: Who am I (individual)? Who we are (organisation)? And where we are going (Organisational focus)? Stories thus give identity to corporate culture and values within and outside the organisation.

Armstrong has offered a new paradigm shift in corporate management by not only making use of storytelling but incorporating contemporary approaches in order to accommodate the postmodernist mindset with the use of every available medium of communication. This has eliminated the drudgery of pulling his staff together every time he wants to celebrate a story within the organisation. The versatility of this approach enhances human participation and a collective sense of belonging at every point of engagement of the work force and the sustenance of the organisational vision and objectives.

The potency of this transformation of bringing past accomplishments, mistakes and stories into perspective has tremendous power to shape today and transform tomorrow. John Drane (2001: 145) sums it up thus:

... Where the story of what is past is not a collection of abstract facts – still less dead historical memories – but something living and lively which can illuminate and reshape the story which is unfolding in the present.

The paradigm shift is not only peculiar to management of corporate business organisations in the use of storytelling, but it has been observed by some consumers that their products often fail to live up to their storyline as the small print of the terms of contract has caused more financial pain than the joy of having their products. Thus to some consumers organisational storytelling, especially in advertising, heightens their suspicion rather than confidence in their products. This attitude, however, cannot be extended to preachers as biblical storytelling has eternal consequences to the preacher and listener. Preachers ought to and should be eternally minded; as such the Gospel should and must not be use as a mechanism for selfish gains or as a manipulative tool.

Most Christian authorities are equally of the opinion that the Gospel should be preached through the storytelling approach in order to break the communication barrier posed by the mindset of the postmodernist. Dan Kimball (2003: 172) puts this in perspective as he notes that:

> Many post-Christian younger people, when they hear explanations of Biblical teaching, including the Gospel of Jesus ... start in the middle of a story they don't know or that they know very little about mainly through negative experiences. We offer them escape from a peril they don't know they face, and we use words that either aren't part of their vocabulary or that they don't correctly understand. Because people in the emerging culture don't know the story, preachers must become storytellers again.

The new 'song' of storytelling within the Christian community is not so new in its entirety as the scripture provides a strong biblical basis for the use of storytelling. Storytelling should be seen as an enviable knowledge management tool that is critical in contemporary communication because we live in a different world; an age when facts are not enough. William Bausch (1984: 128) opines that the concept of absolute truth against which the postmodernist argues is personal. He notes that:

> Truth in the Christian context is not prepositional. Because of its locus in Jesus, it is always personal. The means of communication favoured by Jesus, endorsed by Scripture, and largely forgotten by the church, is that of storytelling.

Storytelling is open and participative. It does not impose itself upon hearers, but invites them to take their own imaginative stance within the structure of the story ... our world is weary of sermons, but hungry for stories. Those who walk the path of the gospel will have plenty of raw material, both from the tradition we have inherited, and from our own experience along the way.

Jesus' approach underscores the fact that communicating a message to an audience which holds strong views can be counterproductive. He knew that answering their entreaties might constitute interference or distortion and, as such, He minimised their prejudice through the power of stories and parables. It is a good tip for biblical communicators, then, to remember that a well-told story about someone else's experience propels listeners to remember who they aspire to be.

There is an old journalistic adage about the difference between a statistic and a tragedy. Two hundred people killed in a plane crash are a statistic. The loss of one life, an eighteen-year-old girl named Jessica headed to Stanford to study nursing, becomes a tragedy. (Johnston 2001: 158)

Stories are marvellous avenues of summarising experiences, capturing an event and the prevailing context that seems essential. Stories are vital cognitive events, as they encapsulate, into one compact package, information, knowledge, context and emotion.

The story we listen to breathes life into stale facts and shows patterns which help us to make connections as they work upon our imagination; pointing to more than meets the eye. It is out to elicit a response from the heart and the head due to the use of images and symbolic language which make us think about life, values, tastes, desires etc. Biblical stories illuminate our thinking about life's imponderables, with God as a point of reference giving an open invitation to possibilities and to live out those possibilities.

Storytelling through preaching, teaching or counselling

strikes a chord within the understanding of the listener. The impact is more than hearing but the subconscious mind is awakened where deeper meaning is registered. Anthony de Mello (1986: 23) provides an example:

> The master gave his teaching in parables and stories, which his disciples listened to with pleasure and occasional frustration, for they longed for something deeper. The master was unmoved. To all their objections he would say, 'You have yet to understand that the shortest distance between a human being and truth is a story.'

Stories are an avenue for men to find meaning to life. Father William Bausch (1984: 34) noted

> we don't tell stories to prove a point or hammer out a lesson, but to disclose a way of looking at life, a way of seeing issues. If you remember, for example, Harper Lee's novel or the film, *To Kill a Mockingbird*, you get an artistic narrative of the way people see blacks and whites, justice and injustice; a way of seeing issues. W. Auden was right in saying, 'You cannot tell people what to do; you can only tell them parables.'

Stories are quite evocative; they resonate in the heart of men beyond the narrator thereby creating a lasting and more effective avenue of communication with congregants.

Chapter 5

Principles of Effective Communication in Storytelling

'Those who do not have power over the story that dominates their lives, the power to retell it, rethink it, deconstruct it, joke about it, and change it as times change, truly are powerless, because they cannot think new thoughts.'

Salman Rushdie

Joe Griffith (2000: ix, xi) in his book, *Speaker's Library of Business Stories, Anecdotes and Humour* asserts that a good story is an integral part of effective communication. He states that:

> gifted communicators have one common denominator: They can tell a story. More to the point, they can use a good story to make a point and to fix that point in the listener's mind ... By sprinkling illustrations ... throughout your presentation, you will grab the imagination of your listeners in a way that films or television are hard pressed to duplicate. Never forget that as a communicator you are appealing to the most powerful image producing mechanism on earth ... the human mind. It thrives on images. Good stories are triggers that release an explosive, powerful, positive form of communication energy.

The preacher's job is made more challenging but yet easier

with the postmodern psyche. The gregarious nature of post-moderns makes the process of defining its values a continuous process of discovery and discernment due to the fluidity of the postmodern mindset. In his book, *Postmodern Pilgrims: First Century Passion for the 21st Century World*, Leonard Sweet uses four adjectives to describe the postmodern mindset which he considers to be a new epistemology, but these adjectives underpin the postmodern's values. His view provides a broad-spectrum appeal in understanding the paradigm shift of the prevailing values of postmoderns in the West. Sweet made use of the acronym 'EPIC'. This acronym reflects four distinct characteristics in which postmodern people interact with their world. It stands for: Experiential, Participatory, Image-driven, and Connected. Amazingly, storytelling provides an avenue for effective communication which can be explored by gospel communicators to reach postmoderns as stories allow the participation of the listener, create connectedness, can be image-oriented and oftentimes appeal to the experience of the listener.

The paradigm shift in culture from modernity to postmodernity has had a multifaceted effect on human psyche which is quite reverberating. There seems to be a general consensus amongst gospel communicators that storytelling is one of the effective tools to reach postmoderns.

Postmoderns are the new breed of thinkers and storytelling has been identified as effective in communicating with this generation of experiential thinkers. Postmodern story thinkers 'have become some of the most creative, productive citizens of society. They want the information and they want it straight. But, they want it in a way that holds their interest. Stories are the best way to reach this new breed of thinker' (Walsh 2003: 16).

The postmodern worldview, which is at variance with the biblical worldview, can be a point of contact with the postmoderns as the communicator of the Gospel sees himself more as a missionary communicator rather a preacher about to declare propositional truth as it was in the modern era. This results in a dynamic interaction with the prevailing culture as such preachers within the postmodern world must and should see themselves as missionaries, even when the prevailing cultural shift has dramatically altered the socio-cultural norm that they grew up with. It is indeed a generational shift. Leslie Newbigin exemplified in his book *Foolishness to the Greeks* his tripartite communication model. His first model recognises that 'communication must first take place in the worldview of the listener, accepting 'at least provisionally, of understanding things that is embodied in that language.' Secondly, engaging such a culture's realities of truth in relation to the gospel truth can lead to repentance of the listeners. And thirdly it must be recognised that this repentance is solely a divine initiative and not due to the communication competence of a preacher. Newbigin (1986: 7) further asserted that

> on the one hand, [the preacher] may simply fail to communicate; he uses the words of the language, but in such a way that he sounds like a foreigner; his message is heard as the babbling of a man who really has nothing to say. Or, on the other hand, he may so far succeed in talking the language of his hearers that he is accepted all too easily is familiar character – a moralist calling for greater purity of conduct or a guru offering a path to the salvation that all human beings want. His message is simply absorbed into the existing worldview and heard as a call to be more pious or better behaved. In the attempt to be 'relevant' one may fall into syncretism, and in the effort to avoid syncretism one may become irrelevant.

Storytelling creates the much-desired connectedness with the postmodern and as such is a valuable tool for communicating the good news.

The creativity of the storyteller is important in communicating the good news; a story should not be used for its own sake, just because it is a good story to the storyteller, but an effective story must move people beyond the narration. Stories can be recycled and reinterpreted to fit the needs of the moment as perceived by the preacher. The creativity of a storyteller might be limited but he or she can borrow extensively from illustrations of others or recreate their illustrations. However preachers must always acknowledge the source of illustrations and stories as any suggestions of plaglarism might cast aspersions on the integrity of the storyteller or preacher. Raymond Bailey writing in the *Concise Encyclopaedia of Preaching* edited by John Knox observes that:

> The clergy have not escaped the temptation to steal sermons and illustrations. King James found plagiarism so wide spread in Elizabethan England that he issued a decree that every preacher should deliver at least one original sermon per month. Famous preachers such as Cotton Mather, Peter Marshall and Luther King, Jr, have been publicly accused of borrowing freely from others without crediting them.

J. John, British witty master of storytelling creativity, is an excellent point of reference in postmodern storytelling as he makes use of anecdotes, metaphors and stories creatively to illustrate biblical truth. The high point of his creativity is the contemporary relevance of his stories which illustrate biblical truth without compromising the biblical standard. John Byrne, the *Private Eye* cartoonist, comments that J. John's series on the Ten Commandments is an affirmation of the obvious truth about the speaker's creativity and the understanding of the cultural dynamics of Westerners in relation to biblical culture. Byrne describes John as 'a brilliant and witty speaker [who] captures the audience in a wonderful way' and the series [Ten] as 'a resource that would work well – from individuals who want some lifestyle tips, to people who want to know more about God.' This has made the 'Ten' a valuable resource to the churched and un-churched as J. John taught on various challenging issues man is confronted with ranging from how to find contentment, how to hold the truth, how to prosper with a clear conscience, how to 'affair proof' your relationships, how to manage your anger, how to keep peace with your parents, how to stop driving yourself crazy, how to take God seriously, how to know the real and how to live by priorities. A major feature of J. John's creativity was the dexterity with which he avoided the use of church traditional languages as he engaged his audience from a very interesting perspective as he translated the Gospel for his audience. The understanding of the cultural milieu in Jesus' day is quite important in the contemporary application of the scripture. Most of the stories and parables of Jesus had much local colouration as most of the stories' or parables' plots were derived from the cultural background, prejudice, reasoning and mindset of the Israelites and their neighbours. Thus to communicate the good news effectively the historical and cultural context must be understood in order to communicate outside the Palestine audience.

This is very much in consonance with Jesus' model as Jesus spoke to people in an interesting style. Mark 12:37 (New Contemporary version) says, 'the large crowd listened to Jesus with pleasure' while the New International Version says 'they [the crowd] listened with delight'. The preaching that leaves a lasting impact upon the listener is that which has life application which transforms the listener. The whole essence of storytelling the Gospel is to transform our character. As D.L. Moody once said, 'Bible was not given to increase our knowledge but to change our lives.'

There are several principles of storytelling, which form the bedrock of effective communication, some of which include the following:

The principle of openness and participativeness

A fundamental principle of storytelling in effective communication is that the story must be open and participative. The use of story is an automatic invitation to secure the listener's involvement and response as sensitive images and coded messages are seductive in nature oftentimes chronicling daily events or occurrences.

Brown (cited in Shea 1980: 89) said:

> A story must reach me on some level to which I can respond, but it must also 'stretch' me, pull me beyond where I am now, the traditional and fictional reflect concerns and conflict present in our lives and suggest ways of dealing with them.

Brown's perspective sums up the fact that effective communication is attainable via storytelling if the story has relevance to the listener, thereby providing images and ways of thinking. Biblical stories open up our imagination, illuminating our human experiences, giving us insight into possibilities and how to live the possibilities out. For instance from the biblical perspective (2 Sam 12:1–7) Nathan the prophet confronted David about his adulterous relationship with Bathsheba and the murder of Uriah using the parable of two men in one city, one rich and the other poor, where the rich man kills the poor man's only lamb while he has many flocks and herds. In his narration Nathan moved David from the level of a listener to a judge ('As the Lord lives the man who has done this shall surely die!') as he projected himself into the parable; at this point Nathan zeroed in and proclaimed the truth behind the parable to David. Stories have enormous power to move people to reflect over issues. Storytelling, parables and anecdotes are a powerful form of communication as the audience can be projected into the storyline unconsciously through the power of connectedness.

The effectiveness of Nathan's communication was predicated on the following features identified in Nathan's storyline, which are indispensable to a good storyline:

(a) The story was introduced with suspense, as David looked forward to what was next.
(b) The salient points were summarised with clarity of purpose.
(c) The use of vivid imagery was pronounced (lamb, rich

man and poor man], as David was a shepherd and a rich man thus creating connectedness.

(d) There was Personal involvement in the narration.

(e) Nathan didn't stifle the flow of the narration.

Communicating effectively through a story entails the storyteller divulging a little more of the storyline (truth) bit by bit as each step of the passage is revealed. Again, all of this is going on without the story recipient's conscious knowledge that it's happening.

The recipient, though often appearing to be passive, is emotionally and intellectually active, and thus is often unconsciously projected into the storyline. The effectiveness of stories as a communication tool is that they provide the audience with a dramatic journey that offers resolution and fulfilment of life-like issues, events and human needs. Storytellers are not out to plague us (humans) over our past but offer a retrospective avenue to make amends and remember our past in relation to the present and the future, thereby bringing things into our remembrance and providing an avenue for cleansing and being made whole through our confessions.

The ultimate impact of Nathan's story was that David's sin was brought to his remembrance and he sought the mercy of God and received his pardon (Psalm 51).

Storytelling is a way by which the preacher can envision a connection between the biblical Word and the congregation or their stories and the kingdom of God.

Janet Litherland (1991: 3) says:

> Stories have power, they delight, enchant, touch, teach, recall, inspire, motivate and challenge. They help us understand. They imprint a picture on our minds. Consequently, stories often pack more punch than sermons. Want to make a point or raise an issue? Tell a story. Jesus did it. He called his stories 'parables'.

Jesus' approach to communication was through the use of parables and stories. According to the King James translation of the Bible, Mark noted that Jesus 'never spoke without a parable' (Mark 4:33–34) but a perusal of the Bible reveals that Jesus indeed spoke to His disciples without parables! This verse is clarified by examining other versions to ascertain the thought-line of Mark. The *Message* translation clarifies this as it states 'with many stories like these, he presented his message to them, fitting their stories to their experience and maturity'. This invariably places a huge responsibility on the shoulders of any preacher: to assess the experience and maturity of his audience in order to use appropriate stories to communicate the Gospel.

Stories and parables are avenues to teach a natural wisdom of morality, of healing, compassion, values and ethics. Frank Seilhamer (n.d) says

> Parable is a translation ... of two Greek terms that mean 'to throw along side of'. What is involved is a story created to be thrown along side of a true-life situation to drive home the central point the storyteller is trying to make. As Jesus demonstrated, a good picture is worth a thousand words that slip by, illustrated in strokes which a person can visualize, then pin to their memory.

Stories and parables provide insight into truths which are often dressed up by the power of the imagination of the storyteller as truth takes up new garments which the congregants assimilate. Polsky and Wozner (1989: 47) noted the impact of creativity in storytelling through this parable:

> The rabbi was once asked: 'Why does the parable possess such great influence?'
> The magi replied: 'I will explain this by a parable:
> Truth was accustomed to walk about as naked as he was born. No one allowed him to enter a home and everyone who encountered him ran away in fright.
> Truth felt greatly embittered and could find no resting place.

One day he beheld Parable attired in colourful, expensive garments. Parable inquired: "Why are you so dejected, my friend?"

Truth replied: "I am in a bad situation. I am old, very old and no one cares to have anything to do with me."

"Nay," retorted Parable, "it is not because of your age that you are disliked by people. Look, I am as old as you are and the older I grow, the more I seem to be loved. Let me disclose to you the secret of my apparent popularity. People enjoy seeing everything dressed up and somewhat disguised. Let me lend to you my garments, and you will see that people will like you as well."

Truth followed this counsel and dressed himself in the garments of Parable. Ever since then, Truth and Parable walk hand in hand and men love both of them.'

There exists a rich heritage for storytelling historically. Preacher Anne Pellowski (1990: 57) in the chapter 'Religious storytelling' in *The World of Storytelling* noted:

The exemplum is a classic fable or popular anecdote to which has been added a moral ... They were used in sermons, much as parables were used by Christ. The oldest known Christian examples occur in the homilies of Saint Gregory the first (c.600) ... In the thirteenth and fourteenth centuries, certain monks developed the narration exempla into an art that was very successful. This was in large measure due to the example set by the Dominicans and by prelates such as Jacques de Vitry; known to have compiled a number of collections of sermons with stories.

The thirteenth century produced legendary preacher Jacob de Voragine whose collection was known as the *Golden Legendary*. 'His sermons had immense popular appeal, and they were rapidly copied by other preachers into all languages of Europe. The Golden Legend was, next to the Bible, the most popular book of Middle Ages' (Dorcy 1983: 114). The origin of preachers using anecdotes and parables cannot but be traced to Jesus of Nazareth and His disciples. Fr Robert Waznak (1983: 27) describes early Christians as a community of storytellers ... The stories were about Jesus of Nazareth who himself offered such spellbinding stories that they were told and retold and retold by people who found in them a key to their own stories of faith and struggle. The stories of the bible were always retold in a way that noticed the particular needs and concerns of the listeners. Contact with the original story was not lost, but the new listeners found relevance and renewal in the story retold because it involved them in a personal way.

William R. White (1982: 118) says *'we are forgetful people. We need storytellers. We need someone to lay the drama of God's love before us. We need to hear stories of almost-too-good-to-be-true promises of God, the story of the good news in the midst of the world's bad news.'* Storytelling thus opens up the door of mercy. White (1982: 119) narrates the story of a pastor who visited a despondent young man in a country jail and explains how he used storytelling to open up a new worldview to the prisoner:

Once a very bad man died and went before the judgement throne. Before him stood Abraham, David, Peter and Luke. A chilly silence hung heavy in the room as an unseen voice began to read the details of the man's life. There was nothing good that was recorded. When the voice concluded, Abraham spoke: 'Men like you cannot enter the heavenly kingdom. You must leave.'

'Father Abraham,' the man cried, 'I do not defend myself. I have a no choice but to ask for mercy. Certainly you understand. Though you lied to save your own life, saying your wife was your sister, by grace and mercy of God you became a blessing to all nations.'

David interrupted, 'Abraham has spoken correctly. You have committed evil and heinous crimes. You do not belong in the Kingdom of light.'

The man faced the great king and cried, 'Son of Jesse, it is true. I am a wicked man. Yet I dare ask you for forgiveness as you have known it.'

Peter was the next to speak. 'Unlike David, you have shown no love to God. By your acid tongue and your vile temper you have wounded the son of God.'

'I should be silent,' the man muttered. 'The only way I have used the blessed name of Jesus is in anger. Still, Simon, son of John, I plead for grace. Though you walked by his side and listened to words from his own lips, you slept when he needed you in the garden, and you denied him three times in his night of greatest need.'

Then Luke the evangelist spoke, 'You must leave. You have not been found worthy of the kingdom of God.'

The man's head bowed sadly for a moment before a spark lit in his face. 'My life has been recorded correctly,' the man began slowly. 'I am guilty as charged. Yet I know there is a place for me in this blessed kingdom. Abraham, David and Peter will plead my cause because they know the weakness of man and the mercy of God. You, blessed physician, will open the gates to me because you have written of God's great love for the likes of me. Don't you recognise me? I am the lost sheep that the Good Shepherd carried home. I am your younger brother, the prodigal brother.'

And the gates opened and Luke embraced the sinner.

'You see' the old pastor concluded, 'I want you to learn stories, not as an exercise in fiction, but in order to walk in mercy. Stories will help you find you.'

In the use of fictional stories to illustrate the kingdom motif, the preacher must emphasise the kingdom motif at the resolution of the story in order not to end up confusing his audience rather than convincing them.

The import of the pastor's story was to give the despondent young man hope that despite past misdeeds, the door of mercy is still open to him if only he can reconcile with God. It is important to note that the sequence of the pastor's narration is not in line with the biblical account of Judgement as the door of mercy is shut after death. Paul affirms this in the book of Hebrews (9:27) as he noted: 'it is appointed for man to die once and after death there is Judgement'. This is further affirmed in the book of Luke (16:19–25). Preachers should always ensure that stories utilised in the communication of the Gospel do not contradict the doctrine of the scriptures and the morals or values of the stories must be emphasised to the listener.

Principle of creative use of words, images and symbols

Creative use of words, images and symbols by a storyteller is an indispensable tool in effective communication. The degree to which a storyteller masters this art will determine his effectiveness in communication, as this is a major tool of the trade. A storyteller must be versatile in the craft of language, knowing how to create metaphors, evocative descriptions of scenery and strong dialogue just the way a surgeon handles the scalpel. David Abram (1997: 265) succinctly highlights the merits of a well-crafted story as an effective tool for communication as he noted:

> A story that makes sense is one that stirs the senses from their slumber, one that opens the eyes and ears to their real surroundings, running the tongue in the actual tastes in the air and sending chills of recognition along the surface of the skin. To make senses that wake up to where they are.

The effective use of words, images, and symbols gives an open invitation to recipients of the story through the power of language as the listener might respond to his or her grace within the story. There must be variation in sentence structure, vocabulary and imagery while there should be avoidance of awkward repetition of words or confusing sentences. Words have a tremendous impact on a listener and as such a storyteller must be aware of the potency of the use of words. Leo Rosten says, '*words sing. They hurt. They teach. They sanctify. They were man's first immeasurable feat of magic* ...' The use of appropriate words in storytelling has a compelling impact on the listener as they resonate in their heart and mind. In Nathan's narration to David the story would probably have had a different impact on David if Nathan had not mentioned that the rich man killed the **one** little ewe that the poor farmer had. Though the phrase **one little ewe** is just three words, it evoked the feeling of wickedness, cheating and callousness in the heart of David which was the leverage that Nathan utilised in projecting the heinous crime of murder and adultery with Bathsheba to his consciousness: David pronounced judgement on the perpetrator of the deed not realising that God had 'developed the photograph of his sin in his darkroom', presented to him as a story by Nathan.

Words not only convey something but are something as Fredrick Buechner (1982: 68) observes: *'words have colour, depth, texture of their own, and the power to evoke vastly more than what they mean ... that words can be used not merely to make things clear, make things happen inside the one who reads them or hears them.'* He also speaks of 'the great power that the language has to move and in some measure to transform the human heart.' A good story makes use of appropriate words.

Storytelling is quite evocative as it opens up the door for metaphors to operate. Buechner (1982: 68) further noted for example

> ... you describe the apprehension a child experiences in moving to a new school, you must have done more than describe moving to a new school. You have produced a metaphor that touches images of apprehension throughout the congregation. You may not have intended to address the person who is about to retire from the railroad ... and that person may not be able to identify just what the connection was, but impact – however undefined propositionally – happened.'

The essential function of metaphor is provocatively superimposing one set of meanings over another. What it may lack in explicit expression is gained in the creative mixing of disparate images.

In His discourse about His second coming, illustrated with the story of the good man of the house in Matthew 24:42–44, Jesus said that the good man of the house does not know when the thief will come in the night. Jesus left His listeners with a partial description of the events that will unfold at His second coming. The beauty of the illustration is that it does not give a detailed insight to every nuance of the kingdom motif, but generates diverse images in the minds of the listener such as memories of sounds in the dark, the presence of an uninvited guest in the middle of the night and the scary experience and its aftermath. This deliberate approach forces the listener to make connections of meaning and subsequently a new perspective about life. This oftentimes is intentionally done by storytellers in order to allow the listener to discover themselves in the storylines as their imaginations are piqued. This is why C.H. Dodd (1961: 5) once spoke about the art of the parable in this way: 'At its simplest, the parable is a metaphor or simile drawn from nature or common life, arresting the hearer by its vividness or strangeness, and leaving the mind in sufficient doubt about its precise application to tease it into active thought.'

The famous founder of Seventh Day Adventist Church, Ellen G. White* (1941: 17–22), identified five distinctive uses of parables by Jesus Christ which are:

1.   Illustration of kingdom motif

'In Christ's parable teaching the same principle is seen as in His own mission to the world (...) the unknown was illustrated by the known; divine truth by earthly things with which the people were most familiar.'

2.   Introduction of new revelation

'Christ sought to remove that which obscured the truth. The veil that sin has cast over the face of nature, He came to draw aside, bringing to view the spiritual glory that all things were created to reflect. His words placed the teachings of nature as well as of the Bible in a new aspect, and made them a new revelation.'

3.   To awaken inquiry

'Jesus desired to awaken inquiry. He sought to arouse the careless, and impress truth upon the heart. Parable teaching

---

* The author does not subscribe to the teachings of Ellen G. White in totality but agrees with her on the functions of parables in Jesus' discourses.

was popular, and commanded the respect and attention, not only of the Jews, but of the people of other nations. No more effective method of instruction could He have employed.'

4. Broad spectrum appeal

'Jesus sought an avenue to every heart. But using a variety of illustrations, He not only presented truth in its different phases, but appealed to different hearers. Their interest was aroused by figures drawn from the surroundings of their daily life. None who listened to the Saviour could feel that they were neglected or forgotten.'

5. To Protect His message and ministry

'And He had another reason for teaching in parables. Among the multitudes that gathered about Him, there were priests and rabbis, scribes and elders, Herodians and rulers, world-loving, bigoted, ambitious men, who desired above all things to find some accusation against Him (...) The Saviour understood the character of these men, and presented truth in such a way that they could find nothing by which to bring His case before the Sanhedrin. In parables He rebuked the hypocrisy and wicked works of those who occupied high positions, and in figurative language clothed truth of so cutting a character that had it been spoken in direct denunciation, they would not have listened to His words, and would speedily have put an end to His ministry.'

Jesus' parabolic sayings were intriguing as most of them had open-ended qualities and as such most His listeners never knew what He meant. This stems from the fact that He did not want to forestall the active participation of the listener's thought. This approach was not peculiar to the listeners alone but also His disciples as He rarely explained the parables to them (Mark 4:13; 7:17–18).

The underlying principle behind the use of metaphors is that they are not finished ideas that do not require the active participation of listeners but a process crafted so that we can speak about the experience, not simply of listening to parables, but of '*being parabled* – of being seized and twisted into new form by its very incompleteness', that creates the completeness of the story as the listener actively engages in finding meaning to the story and its implications (Topel 1976: 10–17) .The use of parables by Jesus was part of a total programme of second-order change. The listener is pressed to discover some thread of similarity amid great dissimilarity, as he is engaged in a fervent quest for meaning that reorients his thought and way of life.

This is due to the fact that Jesus uses language *against* language. Most of His parables have the uniqueness of altering the thought and speech by engaging the listener's worldview. He often opens up a new fountain of grace as truth is unravelled for the listeners as they are forced to question the purpose of such iconoclastic language.

The use of imagery and metaphor is not limited to story-telling any more; Sallie McFague (1982: 34) observes how science is forced to turn to story, imagery and metaphor to describe its work:

> When we turn to the sciences, whether mathematics or the natural or social sciences, we also find metaphor to be central. Perhaps it is most surprising to those who suppose that metaphor belongs only in the arts and religion to discover it at most basic level in mathematics: the numerical monologue. Seeing the similar number among otherwise disparate entities is a metaphorical act, as six apples, six moons, six ideas, and six generous acts. In the social sciences the ubiquity of metaphor is obvious: the human being has been seen as a child of God, as half-angel and half-beast, as a machine; the state has been viewed as an organism and a mechanism; the brain has been understood through the metaphor of the computer and vice versa. When one turns to physics, the evidence of the importance of metaphor in the form of models is extensive ... Jacob Bronowski speaks for many philosophers of science when he insists that ideas in science, as in any other field are derived from images ...

Our culture today is a visual one, an age of '*picture think-*

ing'. The multimedia nature of postmoderns cannot be ignored. Ironically there exists a lot of visual language on the pages of the scriptures in both the Old and New Testament as God revealed Himself in a narrative and visual language. Jesus was not an exception as He used visuals and picturesque language. Preachers must not forget that we live in 'age of visual language' (Lewis and Lewis 1983: 10). To ignore this feature is a 'culpable' act for a preacher as a preacher must be interested not only in delivery of the message but see that the message is communicated effectively. Preachers can effectively communicate the gospel through storytelling by making use of fitting illustrations, word pictures, vivid imagery and even multi-media elements within a story. In 2005, in one of my sermons on the power of imagination, I made use of the story of England International and Liverpool football club captain, Steven Gerrard, to illustrate the inherent power of imagination. Prior to the European Champions League final match in 2005 against AC Milan, Gerrard said, 'I went to the hall of fame and looked at the trophies and victory celebrations and I imagined I would carry the trophy rather than Paolo Maldini.'

The words did not connect with my audience but as soon as the multimedia clips of the victory celebration were shown on the screen the audience became uncontrollable with a great sense of connectedness with the illustration. Though my audience identified with my illustration, amazingly I was ministering to Africans in Diaspora in the United Kingdom which implies that Africans in Diaspora are gradually imbibing the culture of their host as watching football in the United Kingdom is almost like attending church during the Wesleyan Revival!

A perusal of all parables and stories utilised by Jesus during His earthly ministry is best described as a lock and key mechanism in which there is a high level of connectedness with His audience; as virtually all His metaphors and allusions in the storyline were not alien to the Jewish cultural practices of His days. As such the stories and parables became a vehicle for them to see to things from a different perspective as 'their understanding would thus more easily and clearly recognise these truths, they would embrace them with greater firmness and decision, and their memory would retain a deeper and more lasting impression of them' (Fonck 1998: 26). Most of the characters, activities, locations, metaphors, similes and the idiosyncrasies depicted by various characters in Jesus' stories and parables were drawn from nature and common life. For instance the parable of the vine and the vinedresser in John 15:1 is a very good illustration of this view. The image of the vine and the vinedresser was pertinent as these were major features of the Palestine agrarian economy. Henri Daniel-Rops (1962) observed that 'the Old Testament compared the chosen people to it [a vine], nor by hazard Jesus likened Himself to the vine, and made of wine the tangible symbol of His blood'. Jesus' approach in this use of the vine was to bring about reflective thinking in His Jewish audience, who were very conversant with the significance of the vine dating back to the prophetic books of Isaiah (5:1–7), Jeremiah (2:21) and Hosea (10:1).

In the scripture the vine had been used in various contexts, for instance the Psalmist used it as the image representing the nation of Israel in Psalm 80:8, 'Thou didst bring a vine out of Egypt; thou didst drive out the nations and plant it.' This passage is with reference to the deliverance of the nation of Israel from the clutches of Pharaoh and the host of Egypt, while in Ezekiel 19:12 the context of the usage was with respect to coming Judgement.

The assertion made by Jesus as the 'true vine' is connotative and distinctive as the adjective clarifies that He is the authentic vine. The term 'true' (Greek: *alethine*) is translated as 'dependable, genuine'; the basis of this emphasis is to distinguish Jesus as the authentic vine. This view is further corroborated by the usage of the vine in the Gospel of John as the basis of comparison of truthfulness from falsehood (John 1:9; 4:23; 6:32; 7:28; 8:16; 17:3; 19:35). Thus Jesus was declaring the supremacy of His Lordship in contrast to any other false Messiah. Jesus was able create a palpable interest in the kingdom motif as His listeners knew that without the vine, the branches cannot do anything. Jesus was extremely imaginative in His parabolic sayings: His ability to present the mystery of God through images drawn from the world of nature to emphasise divine rule is still very much unparalleled in history.

The principle of dramatic elements in a story

Effective communication is attainable through storytelling by understanding the dynamics of structure in storytelling. The truths of the story are arranged by a storyteller to create a dramatic movement towards the fulfilment of the story to its audience. In *Romeo and Juliet* the opening scene is the confrontation between the Capulets and the Montagues in the streets of Verona due to hatred for one another.

Due to the fact that *Romeo and Juliet* is about the power of love, Shakespeare thus sets forth in the opening scenes what kind of action generates opposition to the story's resolution (hatred). The story sets out to demonstrate the magnitude of the love required in order to overcome hatred. The dramatic structure of the elements sets out what the storyline is all about. The Wikipedia online encyclopaedia noted that Shakespeare's 'use of dramatic structure, especially his expansion of minor characters and use of subplots to embellish the story, has been praised as an early sign of his dramatic skill. The play ascribes different poetic forms to different characters, sometimes changing the form as the character develops. Romeo, for example, grows more adept at the sonnet form over time. Characters frequently compare love and death and allude to the role of fate.' A very good use of dramatic elements gives an overview of a story, giving a preview of what is at stake. Preachers should, however, exercise restraint in the use of overly dramatic elements in a story as the audience might remember the story but forget the kingdom motif behind the story.

The effectiveness of a story as a medium of communication should be built on the arrangement of the elements of the story. For instance in the story of Nathan to David, the roles of the story's characters (the rich shepherd and the poor) were generally defined around how their actions resolved the issue at the heart of the story.

Likewise in the story of the Good Samaritan, crime was committed at an early stage. The roles of the story's characters (the priest, the Levite, the Samaritan) clearly defined how their actions resolved the issue at the heart of the story. Irony is a common feature of most of Jesus' stories. Irony is a complex dramatic form that ranges from simple word play to complex dramatic situations in which things are a reversal of what they seem to be. The Wikipedia online encyclopaedia further defines irony as: 'a literary or rhetorical device, in which there is a gap or incongruity between what a speaker or a writer says and what is generally understood (either at the time, or in the later context of history). Irony may also arise from a discordance between acts and results, especially if it is striking, and seen by an outside audience.' Stories told by Jesus were intrinsically ironic and the writers of the Gospel effectively utilised irony. Luke made use of situational or dynamic irony with no use of verbal irony. The parable of the Good Samaritan has two situational ironies but no verbal irony. The encounter of Jesus with the jurist is documented by Luke in chapter 10:25–37 during the Judean ministry of Jesus.

25 On one occasion an expert in the law stood up to test Jesus. 'Teacher,' he asked, 'what must I do to inherit eternal life?'
26 'What is written in the Law?' he replied. 'How do you read it?'
27 He answered: '"Love the Lord your God with all your heart and with all your soul and with all your strength and with all your mind" and, "Love your neighbour as yourself".'
28 'You have answered correctly,' Jesus replied. 'Do this and you will live.'

29 But he wanted to justify himself, so he asked Jesus, 'And who is my neighbour?'
30 In reply Jesus said: 'A man was going down from Jerusalem to Jericho, when he fell into the hands of robbers. They stripped him of his clothes, beat him and went away, leaving him half dead. 31 A priest happened to be going down the same road, and when he saw the man, he passed by on the other side. 32 So too, a Levite, when he came to the place and saw him, passed by on the other side. 33 But a Samaritan, as he travelled, came where the man was; and when he saw him, he took pity on him. 34 He went to him and bandaged his wounds, pouring on oil and wine. Then he put the man on his own donkey, took him to an inn and took care of him. 35 The next day he took out two silver coins and gave them to the innkeeper. "Look after him," he said, "and when I return, I will reimburse you for any extra expense you may have." 36 Which of these three do you think was a neighbour to the man who fell into the hands of robbers?' 37 The expert in the law replied, 'The one who had mercy on him.' Jesus told him, 'Go and do likewise.'

In the context of the above account of Luke, Jesus encountered a lawyer (in Greek *nomikos*, meaning 'legal expert, jurist, lawyer') a man skilled in interpreting the Jewish Torah (which is the five books of Moses – the Pentateuch). This man who was schooled in the intricacies of the interpretations of the Torah, and his motive was established by Luke as 'to test Jesus'. The Greek word is *ekpeirazo*, 'put to test, try, tempt'. The motive of the jurist might have been to test the theological knowledge of the 'unschooled Galilean lay teacher' but instead of Jesus answering the question of the lawyer, He appealed to the self-perception of the jurist as He asked him 'What is written in the Law?' and 'How do you read it?' (Luke 10:26). In essence Jesus meant 'You are an authority on the Torah. What is the position of the law on the issue at stake?' The legal expert's response in Luke 10:27 was in agreement with Jesus' own assessment of the Torah's message: 'Love the Lord your God with all your heart and with all your soul and with all your strength and with all your mind' which Jesus affirmed, 'You have answered correctly'. But this was dramatic irony as Jesus now assumed the role of the expert on the law commenting on the appropriateness of the comments of the jurist!

In order to defend his legal position, the jurist sought to define words. He asked Jesus what His concept of 'neighbour' was. Neighbour amongst Jews is interpreted as meaning one who is near, in terms of the same religious affiliation and culture (Matthew 5:43–48). The jurist thus placed a limitation on the scope of the usage of the word 'neighbour' as he posited that it was applicable to the Jews only. Jesus knew the intent and the underlying facts of the submission of the jurist but responded by the use of a parable. Parables are stories told to clarify a point which enables listeners to identify with the characters of the story and grasp spiritual truth.

In storytelling it is quite important that the characters have dramatic elements. In this story we have the Samaritan, a wholly unexpected character sequence in the story outline. The descending sequence of Priest – Levite – Israelite ought to be the norm to organise such a story, which is starting from the top of the religious pyramid of the Jewish hierarchy. This sequence is religiously divergent to the Jewish tradition as the hearers would be expecting a Jewish layman to be the third character: this expectation is in conformity with other stories where three people or situations are found in similar stories of that type (Luke 19:11–27; 14:18–20).

The Samaritan was an ironic character as the Jews viewed the Samaritans as half breeds and heretics: though they believed in the Torah, they worshipped at Mount Gerizim rather than Jerusalem (John 4:20–22). The temple at Gerizim was completed at the end of the Persian period (400 BC) but the Jews believed that there was no need for a competing sanctuary. For Jesus to have introduced a Samaritan as a caring person after the priest and the Levite had neglected mercy was well constructed criticism of what passed for 'mercy' among the pillars of Judaism. The jurist could not speak the name 'Samaritan' in response to Jesus' question and he certainly would not have used the adjective 'good' (10:37). The cultural understanding of 'Samaritan' to the lawyer created ironic tension in the story in comparison to his long-held religio-cultural conception of a Samaritan.

The second dramatic irony was that the incident revolved around the jurist in the larger story. The starting point was the jurist's desire to test the young Galilean preacher's theology but he got more than he bargained for as Jesus turned the tables on him. Irony emerges here from the difference in the knowledge of the hearers and the dramatic elements of the story. The jurist kept on acting in his perceived interest but every act of his plunged him deeper into a difficult position as the 'untrained young Galilean' preacher was forced to admit that he knew the one who had the mercy (10:37). Jesus further heightened the 'humiliation' of the jurist as He instructed him, 'Go and do likewise.' The teacher of the law was instructed by Jesus not only to learn from the Samaritan but to show mercy like the Samaritan. What an incredible irony of great dramatic elements.

In the use of storytelling in communicating the gospel truth to the postmodern generation, it is quite important for communicators of the Gospel to have a wide range of understanding of cultural and religious sensitivity of their listeners in mind. This is because social, cultural and religious barriers might become signposts for unravelling divine truth.

It is a regrettable observation that amongst some preachers and Evangelists the use of bad illustrative stories that fail to have been very well thought out in making a point have left the story incomplete and the audience open to fresh areas of confusion. A story is good, but exaggeration is an act of dishonesty and as such sinful. Parables do, however, have an open-endedness.

The principle of plot in storytelling

A preacher who understands what a plot is in storytelling has laid the foundation for creating one. A plot is the process of generating questions in and around the outcome of a story's purpose that gives the story a dramatic and fulfilling element to an audience. A major feature of the storytelling by Jesus in the scripture is the establishment of the basic outline of His stories in the first verse – which, if read, might not be more than 10 seconds (Matthew 13:31). The opening verse presents a skeletal outline of the story-line which invariably connects with the introduction of the characters, the setting, the role of the characters and the interplay of the characters to generate the kingdom motif Jesus was exploring.

A plot is the overall arc of a story. It is what happens in a story, which includes character actions and external events that happen to the characters. A plot is a cause and effect, a logical progression of events in a story. The classic dramatic structure of a plot in storytelling is that the plot has three parts: a beginning, middle and end. The plot of a story makes a story visible and establishes its dramatic movement. The potency of plot in a story is dual: it makes the movement of a story dramatic and it facilitates the incorporation of what is at stake in the story, while plot-generated events block the actions of the characters. In a story with a good plot as the character faces increasing struggles, they must strive with greater purpose to shape the outcome: this generates heightening of a story's movement to fulfilment.

A storyteller who aims to communicate effectively must set up the plot of his story by introducing the characters and setting, communicating the situation from which the story emanates, and then present a tension build-up which often challenges the character in an unexpected manner. The climax of the build-up creates a fulfilment or resolution of the story for the audience.

A very important key in a story plot is motion. The storyteller must keep the story in motion from the set up, and build it up, as the build-up of the story not only escalates the tension but keeps the audience in suspense until the final fulfilment. A story might lose its appeal if it is devoid of motion, action and change.

In the creation of the story plot, the storyteller should highlight significant consequences in the world of the characters, which should reflect throughout the story, and this can only be anchored through coherence of the various subplots that are central to movement of the story.

The principle of unity, coherence and emphasis

Unity, coherence and emphasis are the tripod on which storytelling rests as an effective tool in communication. Taking a cue from the advertising industry and the media, in telesales, the advertiser mentions the name of the product, and the telephone number to call, over and over again.

The advertiser has just one message which must not get muddled up with other adverts. In a similar vein, a story can only be an effective tool for communication if it does not get muddled up with themes outside the overall theme. Many storytellers fail to communicate effectively as they may have many wonderful ideas but lack a unifying message to take home.

It is not the amount of themes that a storyteller generates in a story that is important but it is the ability to consistently integrate all the ideas into an overall theme that determines the effectiveness of the storyteller, as many ideas are often left hanging, with too many images left undeveloped.

Brevity and the development of a single idea will be greatly more effective than a story with several trains of thought. The recipe for unity in a storyline is just to keep it as simple as possible. Each word and sentence must lead the listener towards a greater understanding of the overall theme or controlling idea, and then the story is unified – it exhibits unity.

Preachers need to exercise restraint in the use of story in homilies as:

> Sometimes preachers [have] such a good and captivating story – or a joke – that they can't discipline themselves and simply must tell it because it's so good. But if it is not germane, save it for another time. Else people get caught in distracting delight of the story and can't move on to the topic of your homily. (Bausch 1996: 64)

The ability of a preacher to understand the dynamics of incorporation of story into homilies is predicated on his timing skills, brevity of the story and the relevance of the story to the homily, which often increases with the maturity of the preacher in the ministry.

Coherence means all the puzzles in the story must fit together. There must be an 'enzyme substrate reaction' in which all the ideas or themes raised in a story are connected. This lock and key mechanism is only attainable if the ideas generated in the story are interwoven and dependent on one another, and should be a reflection of the overall theme of the story. An effective story in communication can be compared to a piece of fine cloth; it seems to the listener that the threads have been woven together from words in a way that creates a perfect piece of material with no 'loose threads'.

The opening lines of the parable of the prodigal son according to the Gospel of Luke chapter 15:1–32 shows a high degree of coherence as the author noted 'There was a man who had two sons'. From this brief introduction of the parable the underlying principle of comparability of two characters is put in motion. This invariably is reflected in further narration of the distinctive behavioural pattern of the two sons as the whole storyline can be divided into two sections (Luke 15:11–24 and 25–32) to reflect the comparability introduced in the opening words of the narrative. The two distinctive narratives about the main characters of the story reveals inner coherence in the storyline as the cause and effect of the actions of the younger son is easily identifiable as the desire for independence from the love and affection of his father, the consequences of his actions and his repentance. Jesus employed a high degree of vividness and a deep understanding of Jewish culture in narrating the degree of permissiveness of the younger son as He used images such as 'asked for his inheritance', 'journey into a far country', 'joined himself to a citizen of the country', 'feed swine', 'husks that the swine did eat'. All these descriptions contravened the Jewish moral and religious etiquette of His day, for instance the prevailing Roman–Jewish worldview of Jesus' day would not permit the father to make arbitrary disposal of his estate, and to work in a pig pen was considered one of the most degrading employments, not only by the Jews but by other nations at that time. Jesus used this image to paint the magnitude of the depravity and misery of sinners (the young man) and their captivity by the power of sin. It is imperative to realise that this particular parable was utilised by Jesus to illustrate the pharisaic attitude towards repentance and as such it is allegorical.

The inner coherence of this narration is seen in the distinctive reoccurrence of similar phrases in the parable such as the young 'man woke up' from his servitude in the pig pen and he said 'father I have sinned against heaven and against you. I am no longer worthy to be called your son, make me like one of your hired men'. Similar words are repeated at his reunion with his father with the exception of the last clause ('make me one of your hired men') as the restorative gestures of his father (hug, kiss, signet, robe, shoe,) are not suggestive of a slave but of a son. Similar reoccurrence is noted in phrases such as 'killed the fattened calf', 'dead and His alive again', and 'lost and his found'. These appear at the end of the first part (verse 24) and reoccur at the resolution of Jesus' narration in verse 32 which emphasised the climax of the narration.

Emphasis does not only entail voice inflection but the way we place sentences and words which was quite evident in the parable of the prodigal son. For instance, 'The loss of twin babies, Jessica and Jasmine, aged two years old, during the rescue operation after the floods in Gloucestershire becomes a tragedy' is more decidedly emphatic than 'Jessica and Jasmine a set of twins aged two years died'. The ability of a storyteller to emphasise a metaphor, a symbol or specific language in the plot of the story is predicated upon the image or symbol utilised.

The two main subdivisions of the parable show interdependence in Jesus' narration as Luke 15:11–24 is dependent on verses 25–32 to bring about a deeper comprehension of the basis of the comparison set in the opening verse of the parable. The height of the coherence in this narrative is that Jesus devoted a great deal to the attitude of the three characters in the parable i.e. the father, the younger son and his older brother as there was high degree of coherence from one character to another, vivid use of socio-cultural images and a unique resolution hinged on the primary focus: to illustrate God's perspective on repentance in comparison to the pharisaic disposition. That the son who left, and squandered his goods, was rejected, repented, was accepted, received goods and was restored speaks about the restorative act of God to a sinner (Luke 15:24, 32). Some of Jesus' parables were without any end stress: for instance in the parable of the prodigal son we are not told what the older brother did – whether he joined the father in the celebrations or stayed away from the festive gathering. Likewise in the case of the immoral woman who anointed Jesus and was pardoned of her sins: the writer of the book of Luke is silent on Simon's action based on Jesus' words (Luke 7). It has been suggested that the motive of the inconclusive ending of these parables was to create a sense of evaluative approach: for Jesus' listeners to internalise the story and come up with their views on the kingdom motif He explored.

The seemingly inconclusive discourse of the prodigal son was based on the fact that those listening to the story were Pharisees and teachers of the law, who are portrayed in the story by the critical and legalistic disposition of the older son. They were invited to join the festive gathering of the forgiven son who personified the tax collectors and moral outcasts despised by the Pharisees.

The principle of focus

Having a strong grasp of how best to present a story's focus can be a struggle for an inexperienced storyteller in preaching as it is pivotal to effective communication due to the subjective interpretations of listeners. Different people can easily arrive at rather different interpretations of the same story unless the storyteller:

(a) clearly explains his focus;
(b) provides a consistent transition from one idea to another in the storyline;
(c) explains the language or structure.

Many inexperienced storytellers struggle with focus on issues because they shift their focus to make a story seem fresh and engaging but a listener needs to be able to internalise a story's movement. If a listener is unable to internalise a story's movement as a result of changes in focus, the resultant effect is that the listener might be jarred out of the story. A clearly defined focus in storytelling is a very potent tool for effective communication.

One of the largest prayer meetings in the United Kingdom, organised under the auspices of the Redeemed Christian Church of God, and tagged 'Festival Life', is fast becoming a melting point in Christian circles as Charismatics, Evangelicals, Pentecostals and Orthodox Christians gather for an all-night session of prayer, teachings and prophetic proclamations to the congregants. The chief host, Pastor E.A. Adeboye in one of his illustrations on divine guidance, narrated a personal story. He is a preacher who engages in narrative preaching using his personal stories, understood amongst Pentecostals as testimonies for exegesis.

He said:

> God can use the anything to guide you out of trouble. I have experienced God's guidance many times. I was raised up in a town that some you know, Ifewara, and I had an aunty who was living far away from my parents. I wanted to visit my aunty and I had to pass through a forest area. Well you don't have forest in England [laughter from the congregants]. Those of you who are from Nigeria, you might understand what forest is like [laughter again from the congregants]. I was alone and reached a crossroads and didn't know where to turn to, but suddenly I noticed a small white dog wagging its tail at me and promptly I followed the dog. The dog guided me to my aunty's place but as soon as I got to the front of my aunty's house the dog disappeared. My aunty was astonished to see me as she couldn't believe that I came alone but I explained to her that her dog guided me home from the forest. She was dumbfounded as she refuted the ownership of any dog. (applause from the crowd). God will intervene in your situation (a resounding 'Amen' from the congregants).

In the above scenario, it is expedient to note that the preacher was using his personal story that occurred in a different socio-cultural setting to illustrate a biblical theme. He was, however, quick to clarify the usage of the word 'forest' which perhaps is a word that most of the congregants were familiar with, but might not have seen one, in order to eliminate misconceptions. He further re-emphasised that Nigerians in Diaspora can identify with his plight which connected with his audience as it was affirmed with thunderous laughter by the congregants. The obvious focus of this story was neither about the forest nor the dog but about the act of being delivered from the perils of the African forest as he clearly demonstrated this at the beginning (God can guide you in any situation). The appearance of the dog is adjudged by the congregants to be a Theophanic experience which is also noticeable at the resolution of the story as his aunty couldn't comprehend how Pastor Adeboye made it through the forest. The difference in the socio-cultural setting of where this act of divine intervention occurred was not much of a problem to the congregants as a greater percentage of the audience were Africans: as such the concept of forest might not be a forgotten one so soon, especially amongst the first generation migrants of African Diaspora. A major feature of a good story is its brevity in a sermon: the above narration was barely less than two minutes and as such the focus of the theme under consideration was maintained.

The main focus of a story usually comes right at the resolution of the story and is referred to as 'end stress'. For instance in the trilogy of the 'parables of the lost', the 'lost things' – a lost sheep, a lost coin and lost son (Luke 15: 1–32) – are real-life possibilities, not just stories. In all these parables Jesus developed various themes, but a careful examination of the parables reveals well-crafted parables that had a well-defined focus. In the parable of the prodigal son, the father of the two responded to a query of the older son in verse 32 by saying, 'we should make merry and be glad: for this thy brother was dead and is alive again and was lost, is found'. Examining the context that necessitated the parable, it was in response to the Pharisees and the scribes complaining about the restorative gestures to sinners as they complained 'this man receiveth sinners and eateth with them' (Luke 15:2).

Jesus had a well-defined focus in the narration of the trilogy of the parables of the lost as each of the parables had the similar end stress in different phrases which conclusively addressed the mercy, grace and love of God to a repentant sinner.

> 'I say unto you likewise there is joy in heaven over one sinner that repenteth, more than over ninety and nine persons which need no repentance.' Luke 15:7

> 'There is joy in the presence of God over one sinner that repenteth.' (Luke 15:10)

> 'We should make merry and be glad, for this thy brother

was dead and is alive again and was lost and is found.'
(Luke 15:32)

It is quite obvious that there was a smooth transition from
one parable to another in the trilogy of the parables of the
lost, as the resolution of each parable is well stressed and
He continued the second parable with a rhetorical question
and continued straight on to his narration which depicted
God's concern in comparison to the Pharisees murmuring
over the salvation of a lost soul (*The Dake Annotated
Reference Bible*). This was further heightened by the third
parable as the end stress of the older son was a re-enactment of the attitude of the Pharisees towards Jesus'
restorative gestures to the saved. The explanation of the
father of the two sons to his older son was more a reference
to the Pharisees to drop their legalism and critical disposition to celebrate what God has done for the repentant
sinners. It was an indirect invitation to the Pharisees to
have a rethink of their comments as stated in verse 2 of
Luke chapter 15.

The principle of characters

The role of the characters in a story is important as they
operate to make the story's movement visible and concrete.
This must happen if a listener or audience is to desire to
internalise the story's movement toward its fulfilment. The
storyteller, then, needs to be able to make the subtle distinction between what the story is about at the introductory
and deeper level of his or her narration.

All characters in well-told stories must have strength of
purpose. A wide range of issues exist such as love, greed,
revenge, compassion, hate or jealousy that a character must
be willing to confront; and overcome whatever obstacles the
story places in their path. Weak characters offer the listener
no reason to internalise the story as their actions are uncer-
tain and unfocused. The listener literally has difficulty
internalising their actions and assigning them meaning.

Characters are the engine-room of a story. The storyteller in writing or narrating a story must ask himself some of the following questions:

(a) Will the readers or audience care about the characters?
(b) Do the characters seem real?
(c) Can the audience or readers identify with the hero in the story?

If the answers to these questions are 'yes', the storyteller would have created empathy through which the audience identifies with the thoughts, emotions and actions of characters and can evaluate themselves consciously and unconsciously in the mirror of the story.

The vividness of the characters utilised by Jesus in all His parabolic sayings and stories is appropriate as most of the characters are easily identifiable in the socio-cultural setting of the Jews: as such it was memorable to the listeners. Characters like The Farmer in the parable of the Sower, the Good Samaritan, The Priest, The Levite, The Ten Virgins, The Pharisees and the Tax Collector, The Unjust Judge etc. would have resonated in the hearts of the listeners as the Jewish audience were quite conversant with the socio-economic antecedents of the characters in Israel at the time of Jesus. Jesus more or less was engaged in enacting living characters to His audience. Not only were these characters memorable, but the actions of the characters were the basis for illustrating the expected kingdom truth in comparison to the reality of Jesus' days. Interestingly, in the story of the Good Samaritan Jesus exhibited His sense of understanding of the Jewish prejudice against the Samaritans and as such He used the power of irony to jolt His Jewish hearers, by depicting their age-long prejudice and shattering it before their eyes to illustrate the truth of the Gospel.

The principle of connectedness

A storyteller has to create a link with the audience with a positive controlling idea no matter how condensed the story might be. A story that connects with the audience creates powerful images in the mind of the listener. When a story connects with the listener's goals and intentions, the listener will move past the original intentions of the story-teller and achieve more than his or her expectations. This thus establishes participation and an inverse relationship by which the comments of the listener can be utilised by the storyteller to enhance the storyline or bring the story to its fulfilment.

The experience of the General Overseer of the Redeemed Christian Church of God, Pastor E.A. Adeboye in one of his numerous trips to the Western world is a point of reference. He sat by the side of a man on the plane whose dress code quite obviously singled him out as being wealthy. While on board, Pastor Adeboye was eager to preach to his co-traveller but as he looked at the man he knew he lacked nothing materially but salvation. His concern was the point of engagement to initiate a conversation. The only point of engagement was business so he said: 'I want to introduce to you my father, in fact my father is the richest man on earth,' and the businessman next to him was suddenly awakened. He asked, 'What kind of business is he into?' Pastor Adeboye responded, 'He is into petroleum, agriculture and has huge financial investments in gold and silver.' The man was delighted and eager to know more.

The aftermath of this story eventually led to an extended conversation with this businessman. This approach shows the ability of Pastor Adeboye to identify the area of this man's interest which became a point of engagement to minister the Word of God to him. Interestingly, the father in the context of Pastor Adeboye's usage is the Lord. According to Psalm 24:1 'The earth is of the Lord, its full-ness thereof and all that dwelleth therein'. Psalm 50:10 states, 'For every beast of the forest is mine, and the cattle upon a thousand hills,' while Hagai 2:8 says, 'the Gold and Silver are mine'. There seems to be urgent need for preachers to tell the story of salvation all over again as most of the people that are yet to come to the saving grace of Jesus don't have any clue about the biblical worldview.

The transition from the modern era to a postmodern era poses a grave challenge to the Church in its mission 'as the gospel must be constantly forwarded to a new address because the recipient is repeatedly changing place of residence ... unless we work out where they are; we will all fail to communicate with them' (Helmet Thickle cited in Johnston 2001: 16). An in-depth understanding of postmodernity doesn't mean that the Christian message has to be adulterated and this perhaps is the greatest tension that the contemporary Church is faced with. Stanley Grenz (1996: 16) observes that 'Confronted by this new context, we dare not fall into the trap of wistfully longing for a return to the early modernity that gave evangelicalism its birth, for we are called to minister not to the past but to the contemporary context, and our context is influenced by post-modern ideas.' The clarion call for the Church to be relevant in communication of the Gospel in the postmodern context is further espoused by Stanley Grenz (1996: 16) as he noted that 'it would be tragic if evangelicals ended up as the last defenders of the now dying modernity; to reach people in the post-modern context, we must set ourselves to the task of deciphering the implications of postmodernism for the Gospel'. This is very important because the beliefs of the people in the pew are not far from the beliefs of the unchurched. Graham Cray uses the Pauline perspective in 1 Corinthians 9:19–22:

> 'For though I be free from all men, yet have made myself servant unto all, that I might gain the more. And unto the Jews I became as a Jew, that I might gain the Jews; to them that are under the law, as under the law, that I might gain them that are under the law; To them that are without the law, (being not without law to God, but under the law of Christ,) that I might gain them that are without the law; To

the weak I became as weak, that I might gain the weak; I made all things to all men, that I might by all means save some.

To describe the kind of mission strategy the Church should deploy if it is to communicate the gospel in a post-modern world, he affirms that 'if the cross is the heart of the gospel message, the incarnation provides the model for the practice of mission and evangelism'. He goes on to quote New Testament Professor, Morna Hooker: 'Five times over Paul spells out the same theme: he became what others were, in order to win them for the gospel. Five times over he uses the Greek word "gain/win", introduced each time by the Greek word 'in order that' – As far as possible he has deliberately identified himself with those whom he sought to win for the gospel.'

The Pauline perspective of adapting the message to the listener achieved two major things:

(a) an understanding of the mindset of the audience and their perceived needs;
(b) receptivity of the preacher's ideas through the power of identification which is compelled by Christ's love. (2 Corinthians 5:14)

In the postmodern context the communication of the Gospel requires the preacher trading places with the pew (postmoderns) before the other people can level up with the message. Ralph and Greg Lewis (cited in Johnston 2001: 69) agree that 'Meaningful ministry requires more than risking sermons. It means risking ourselves. It means placing ourselves in the pew with our people, admitting our humanness to ourselves and to them, and preaching with the conviction that we all are workers together with God.' The era of proclamation of the Gospel to a non-Jewish audience and with a different worldview in which the preacher fails to identify with the mindset of his target group has progressively come to an end as it is expected that a preacher should live his life out in the community.

The storyteller must eliminate irrelevant details that are foreign or confusing. This is important in order to create a climate of acceptance with a wide range of audiences, as within every story there is a moral, history, or explanation of nature, a teaching or entertainment. The degree to which a storyteller creates connectedness with the listener will determine the effectiveness of his communication effort.

When ministering to the secular people the storyteller must avoid the use of the Church's traditional language that prevents secular people from understanding the good news. Alan Walker (1957: 55–60) discovered this need as a young communicator. After he preached at a Church, a secular visitor requested his sermon notes. The sermon notes were returned to him after several days. He reports:

> He returned the manuscript with each phrase underlined which he did not understand . There were about forty such traditional words and phrases. He wanted to know for example, what 'in Christ' meant ... it brought home to me a lesson I have never forgotten. I believe any Christian who would dare to declare his faith to another must escape from the jargon of his own discipline of thought and make his gospel intelligible by the use of relevant, freshly minted expressions of truth.

The same truth highlighted above is as true of storytelling. The ability of a storyteller to understand the dynamics of the worldview of his audience determines his communication effectiveness. For instance, the accounts of the paralysed man in the Gospels of Mark and Luke. The Gospel of Mark is a primitive Gospel, written for a Palestinian audience. Mark's account notes that the paralysed man was lowered through a roof of thatches, but Luke recorded this same story from another perspective, without changing the structure of the story or its content but with a recognition of the worldview of the Grecian audience. Luke thus changed a detail: 'the man was lowered through the roof tiles' that the Grecians were familiar with.

Storytelling thus becomes an effective tool in communication if the story accommodates the religious and socio-cultural values of its audience without contradicting biblical teachings. The maximum impact of a story is only achievable if the story can be remodelled creatively to accommodate various socio-cultural worldviews. This brings about the emergence of the old truth in a new way; structured to capture the audience's imagination, thus creating a climate of acceptance for the story in the listener.

The avoidance of the use of the Church's traditional language that prevents the understanding of secular people in the pew is very important. The problem of denotation must be avoided in storytelling. The listeners may have no reference at all to 'propitiation' or 'sanctification' or their mind may assign a wrong referent, as when one connects 'kingdom' to King James. The storyteller also must avoid the problem of word connotation as the people that are seated in the pew especially in the Western world might have a different worldview from the biblical worldview: as such to the secular people 'sin' may connote 'sex' and 'love' may connote 'cohabitation.'

In such a scenario, the communicator must employ the most appropriate synonym which the target audience understands. Steve Farrar (1995: 168) in his bestselling book, *Finishing Strong*, creatively re-wrote the biblical story of Moses with a contemporary flavour as he took into consideration his target audience who might have difficulty in understanding the biblical world view.

Farrar's creativity is a reflection of the understanding of the dynamics of Moses' Egyptian educational and socio-cultural background. In order for the narration of Moses' story to have maximum impact on the American audience, he made use of historical and military symbolism in his narration. In the re-enactment of the story, Farrar's imaginative skill was quite obvious: he asserted that Moses was a product of Harvard University where he studied and was awarded a Masters in Business Administration, followed by a PhD from Yale University. The obvious objective of the writer was to pique the imagination of his audience with the idea that Moses had the best training available within the Ancient Egyptian educational system (Harvard and Yale Universities were rated as the first and second best universities in the world according to *The Times Higher Education* rankings of 2007). F.B. Meyer (1983: 157) describes Moses' educational instruction as at the 'Oxford of Ancient Egypt'. This was a result of the adoption of Moses as grandson to Pharaoh; this invariably became the precursor for the educational attainments of Moses. Griffith and Newberry (1894: 40), cited in the *Illustrated Bible Dictionary* edited by Douglas *et al.* (1980: 1026), noted that, 'anciently, children of harim-women could be educated by the Overseer of the harim [a teacher of the children of the king's household]'. This conferred on the children of the king the privilege of having the best educational instruction. This education was structured to reflect the socio-economic and historical requirement of the Egyptian royals, and 'in due course princes were given a tutor, usually a high official at a court or a retired military officer close to the king' (Brunner cited in Douglas *et al.* 1980: 1026). Moses must have acquired much military skill from his retired military instructor during his tutelage, which became evident in his later accomplishment as a general in Pharaoh's army. This implies that Moses' educational training was holistic and a reflection of the need for royal antecedents of the Egyptian kings to meet the military, historical and socio-economic needs for future governance.

The beauty of the creativity of this perspective is the creation of an American world view to replace the Egyptian historical-cum-cultural background of the narration that most Americans might not connect with immediately. According to Finis Dakes, in his annotated Dakes Bible, 'Egyptians were the most intelligent and best instructed people on earth. This learning consisted of the mysteries of Egyptian religion, poetry, music, medicine and hieroglyphics.' This is further affirmed in Stephen's retrospect of the

Israelites' history when he states that 'Moses was learned in the wisdom of the Egyptians and was mighty in words and deeds' (Acts 7:22). Farrar's perspective was with a ring of contemporary relevance as he associated the military training and exploits of Moses with the Second World World War. This allusion was later clarified – nevertheless the basis of his reference was as a result of the military exploits of Moses ['mighty in words and deeds'] in Egyptian history. The Jewish historian, Josephus recorded that Moses was a successful general who led Pharaoh's army to victory over the kingdom of Ethiopia, which had conquered most of Egypt. Josephus asserted that Moses was a great strategist in his conquest of Ethiopia as:

> "... he [Moses] came upon the Ethiopians before they expected him; and, joining battle with them, he beat them, and deprived them of the hopes they had of success against the Egyptians, and went on in overthrowing their cities, and indeed made a great slaughter of these Ethiopians ... the Ethiopians were in danger of being reduced to slavery, and all sorts of destruction; and at length they retired to SABA, which was a royal city of Ethiopia, which Cambyses afterward named MEROE, after the name of his own sister. The place was to be besieged with very great difficulty, since it was both encompassed by the Nile quite round and the other rivers ... (*Antiquities*, II, X, 2)

Farrar's approach in communicating Moses' story was not only creative in style but was deeply rooted in biblical history. The ability to communicate the good news through storytelling should not be limited to biblical sources alone but there exist vast extra biblical sources that provide historical and cultural facts about Bible characters, traditions and customs that can be use in weaving the plot of the storyline.

The use of extra biblical sources as secondary materials to complement biblical themes, history and culture must not contradict biblical doctrine. There exist diverse sacred books apart from the Bible that some denominations and 'churches' assert are 'divinely inspired' but such sacred books have been criticized by various scholars as deviation from normative orthodox Christian doctrine and are classified as Sectarian movements or cults .*

The story of Moses narrated by Steve Farrar can be utilised from a different perspective depending on the location and the worldview of the target audience. The use of Harvard or Yale University or subway, in recreating the same story for a British audience, will not have maximum impact on the audience, who might not be conversant with these universities in comparison to Oxford University or Cambridge University which are amongst the top league universities in the United Kingdom.

This thus places a huge responsibility on the storyteller to make use of familiar images to give validity to his storyline as this creates connectedness with listeners as they can identify with such descriptions, names of places and images that might be in the storyline. The understanding of the socio-cultural values, religious diversity and economic activities of the listeners are pivotal in the use of storytelling in the communication of the gospel. The use of a familiar medium is necessitated to create maximum understanding of the good news. This is a prominent feature of Jesus' parabolic sayings and stories. The illustrations or metaphors or symbols are part of everyday life experiences as they are the 'natural expressions of a mind that sees truth in concrete pictures rather than conceives it in abstractions' (Dodd 1961: 15–16). Jesus indeed might be classified as the best storyteller that ever lived as He communicated the Gospel to His peasant audience by exploring the close relationship of His audience's experiences with nature and the message of the kingdom. He was a man who understood the social

---

* For detailed studies of such criticism and classifications of such movements, sacred texts, doctrines and religious persuasions, see Walter Ralston Martins, *The Kingdom of Cults* (USA, Bethany House Publishers, 1985); George A. Mather, Larry Nichols and Alvin Schmidt, *Dictionary of Cults, Sects, Religions, and the Occult* (Grand Rapids, Michigan, Zondervan Publishing House, 1993).

setting of his audience; Jesus was born into an artisan family in Bethlehem but grew up in Galilee (Matthew 13:54; Luke 2:4, 51). The social status of Jesus amongst Galileans was queried (Mark 6:3) while Mark noted that He was unable to do many miracles in their midst due to their unbelief. There are two main accounts of the socio-historical life of Jesus: one of the two perspectives noted that Jesus was an artisan – a carpenter but with a cosmopolitan itinerary as He travelled around Sephoris, coming into contact with Hellenistic culture that He became quite familiar with, unlike the natives of Galilee. The later view maintained that Jesus was noted as a village carpenter who made a living by combining village carpentry with agricultural work. Jesus was thus bi-vocational before He started His public ministry. Interestingly, Jesus' bi-vocation skills and job language were dominant in most of His parables and stories. This is illustrated by Jesus' warning to prospective disciples 'No one who puts a hand to the plow and looks back is fit for the Kingdom of heaven' (Luke 9:62). This line of thought is the same in His invitation to the weary and the heavily burdened, 'Take my yoke upon you, and learn from me ... For my yoke is easy and burden is light' (Matthew 11:28–30). The agricultural and carpentry images utilised in the passages were not alien to the agrarian audience He was communicating the kingdom truth with. The obvious implication is that the vocational or professional background of a preacher can readily be an effective tool in communicating the Gospel as he can make use of his professional language to serve as metaphors when communicating the Gospel, in the midst of his professional colleagues, to clarify or illustrate kingdom truth. There seems to be a subtle corruption that is gradually enveloping the mindset of some preachers as they often engage in the use of vain words and illustrations that at best confuse their listeners rather than educate, heal, deliver and transform them. The language of communication and illustration must consistently reflect the socio-economic, cultural and linguistic background of the listeners to create a high level of receptivity as Jesus demonstrated in His preaching days. Any preacher who engages in the use of jargon as illustrations is better assessed as being on an ego trip that will achieve nothing but disillusioned parishioners who were well-informed before the commencement of the homily but were more confused and perplexed at the end of forty-five minutes of self-glorification.

The simplicity of a preacher in terms of the illustrations and metaphors utilised in storytelling is electrifying to an audience as connectedness is birth while a lasting impact is made on the listeners due to the simplicity of the illustration. The likes of Billy Graham, Oral Roberts, John Hagee, Rick Warren and Tommy Tenney all have broad-spectrum appeal to people of diverse socio-economic, racial and linguistic backgrounds as they preach with simplicity and a high degree of connectedness using personal stories, often referred to as testimonies, to illustrate biblical truth.

Preachers today must consistently understand the prevailing culture in order to utilise appropriate illustrations. People in the pew often think that the life of most people in the pulpit revolves round the Bible, church and prayer meetings. One of my parishioners was taken aback when I used Will Smith's movie 'Pursuit of Happyness[Happiness]' in one of my sermons. The film is an effective illustration of the plight of the some postmodernists in coping with the challenge of living their dream. The parishioner said, 'Pastor, so you watch what we watch also?, I responded, 'I watch some of the good things you might be watching, or have watched, but not everything you watch.' He laughed! Preachers are oftentimes perceived as not well informed outside the ministerial task (at least until the emergence of contemporary preachers like Bill Hybels, Rick Warren, Robert Schuller, George Hunter Dan Kimball and the likes) about popular culture, fashion trends, TV programmes and economic developments, but any preacher that is ill informed is living in a virtual world and far from the realities of his day. Jesus communicated effectively because He understood the culture, the language and the prejudices of the people and as such the illustrations He used were relational and identifiable by His audience.

The use of illustrations that are embedded in history that have little or no relevance to a contemporary audience might constitute a barrier to effective communication of the good news as your the audience might not be good students of history. I learnt this lesson in my leadership and mentoring quarterly series when I produced a CD entitled 'Time, the Currency of Life', a masterpiece on time management. A business consultant friend of mine listened to the CD before it was to be marketed and said it was an excellent piece, 'but who knows the 4th Earl of Chesterfield and other men you quoted: people will identify more with names like Bill Gates, Mike Mudrock, Richard Branson, Alan Greenspan, Tony Blair, Bill Clinton, Bill Cosby.' It was a subtle way of telling me that this was commendable but if I use the words of Grace Davis, I was 'believing but not belonging' to the realities of contemporary life. In the words of Rick Warren 'if you want to quote someone don't quote some dead English men'. This is not ethnocentrism – reference to spiritual history is excellent but it must surely be in cloak of contemporary relevance.

A preacher must consistently ask these questions with respect to his audience: Where will 1 be preaching? What kind of people will be there (farmers, tradesman, academicians, the rich or poor)? What is the prevailing local news that can create immediate connectedness with the audience? What are the perceived needs of the people that God wants to address? What are the unique humours of the area?

Every culture has its diversity and likewise humour as a cultural element has its uniqueness. The process of translating a joke into another language might render it less effective than in the original culture. Due to the inherent diversity of culture amongst communities a joke in Lancashire might not be understood and create the desired impact in the south of England, even though both regions are English-speaking communities. The ability of a preacher to be conversant with the cultural background, history, politics, food, pronunciations and popular sayings of the area where he preaches can be a great asset, creating a climate of receptivity through the use of humour.

This Lancashire joke by a preacher who wanted to iden-tify with the northern phonetics of his audience, the majority of whom came to the church's service without their Bibles, is quite illustrative of a very good understand-ing of the people and their phonetics. He said 'Some residents on Threlfall Road, Blackpool had just been issued with their first set of wheelie bins in May 2008 and not many of the residents were quite aware of needing to leave it at the end of their driveway instead of the bin-men coming and collecting their wheelie bin. So, the bin-men had been told for the first few weeks to move bins where appropriate. At 66 Threlfall Road [the preacher's residen-tial address] there was no sign of the wheelie bin, so the man rang the door bell. A middle-aged lady opened the door, and the council worker asked: "Where is ya bin?" [Where is your bin?] The lady responded, "I bin in bed" [I've been in bed]. The bin man retorted "No Where is the wheelie bin?" The lady responded "a while bin in bed ..." [been a while in bed].' The congregants burst into laughter. Though the preacher is a Nigerian his sense of humour had relevance to his audience, but as the congregants were settling down after several minutes of laughter and taunting amongst them as a result of the humour, he asked the congregants "Where are your Bibles and not wheelie bins?" The essence of his connectedness was not only in being humorous, but a subtle way of jolting their conscience to the fact that their Bibles are to be brought and utilised by them in the church and not to be left at home during church services. The preacher demonstrated adequate knowledge of local news in his community as some homes in Blackpool had just got their first wheelie from the council! As a faith leader a broad-spectrum understanding of the local news, economic news, polices, investment opportunities or crime rate are avenues to create leverage and connect with the congregants to posit the relevance of the scripture to challenges, hopes, aspirations, fears and their biblical solutions.

The principle of listening

A Turkish proverb teaches that if speaking is silver then listening is gold. In storytelling, listening is one half of the communication process. Man's inability to communicate is as a result of failure to listen effectively, skilfully and with understanding to another person. Listening is almost a lost virtue in our contemporary times. For a story to be an effective communication tool, the story must be very brief and have relevance for the socio-religious culture of the audience. It has been observed that 'thirty-five percent of the meaning of communication derives from words; the remainder comes from the body language' (Harrison cited in Bolton 1979: 78). This strongly implies that non-verbal nuances such as facial and hand gestures are vital in communicating to the listener and in evaluation of the audience level of involvement in the story.

Man's socialisation success is not only predicated on his ability to communicate verbal and non-verbal cues but also his sensitivity to the non-verbal messages of others. These reinforce, encourage or lead to the enhancement of the storyline as oral language uses more channels of communication such as body, eyes, gesture, face and voice inflection.

The dynamics of listening are very profound and this is reflected in the posture of the listener, which can encourage discourse or serve as a barrier. The positioning of the body during conversations is an instinctive radar that measures the effectiveness of one's listening ability, and the storyteller must be aware of it. For instance, listeners who slump with heads down are not an encouraging sign to the speaker as this depicts a sense of tiredness and indifference. The storyteller must be aware that effective communication is created when the listener, according to Bolton (1979: 34), 'demonstrates a relaxed alertness with the body leaning slightly forward, facing the other squarely, maintaining an '"open" position and situating himself at an appropriate distance from the speaker [storyteller].' This implies that the degree of relaxedness has a positive correlation and is a function of effective listening on the part of the audience, which the storyteller must never lose sight of.

The ability of a listener to position himself or herself in facing the storyteller squarely or at eye level is an act of involvement, especially if the listener is listening to an authority or a person in a position of authority. The underlining principle is that in communication, if the sender [storyteller] discovers that the receiver has poor attending posture, this can be corrected humorously in order for the storyteller to maximise the impact of the story on his audience.

One of the subsets of the dynamics of listening is the attentive silence. In the writings of the preacher in Ecclesiastes, 'there is a time to keep silence, and a time to speak" (Ecclesiastes 3:8) Silence, according to a wise saying, is golden. The Psalmist declares that he 'will keep a muzzle on his mouth and will watch how I behave not allowing my tongue to lead me to sin' (Psalm 39:1).

The Psalmist's perspective resonates with the letter of James as he affirmed, 'silence is putting a bit in the horse's mouth' (James 3:3). Silence is an antidote to a culture of abounding words, as a word-saturated culture abuses the use of words, lessening their power and creative impact in communication. Silence on the part of the listener may be passive in outlook but it also can be an active process in which the listener is engaged in deep thought as an appropriate response to all the cues emanating from the storyteller, demonstrated through his posture of involvement such as eye contact, facial expressions etc.

The storyteller must understand the implication of silence during his narration as silence creates intimacy; 'silence of love is not indifference; it is not merely poverty of something to say. It is a positive form of self-communication. Just as silence is needed to hear a watch ticking, so silence is the medium through which heartbeats are heard" (Luccock cited in Bolton 1979: 49).

The goal of silence of the listener is to understand the content of the storyteller's ideas or proposals; the meaning it has for him and the feelings he has about his experiences. Silence from the listener enables him or her to listen to the sequence of the discourse from the storyteller through the avoidance of frequent questions which encourages disclosure of feelings, emotions etc. It is highly successful if backed up with very good attending skills.

Too much silence can lead to a monologue, which can be frustrating to the storyteller due to non-responsiveness of the listener, which can be a sign of dissociation from the story. There are social expectations about the degree of silence and gaze, and people who do not practice such violate this expectation. The absence of such indicates lack of warmth, interest and involvement from the listener. An important feature of non-verbal communication is that it reveals human attitude, noted Steve Duck (1992: 12):

> These attitudes may be attitudes about self (e.g. conceited, diffident, mousy, shy, humble); attitudes towards the other person (e.g. dominant, submissive, attracted, disliking, hostile, aggressive); or attitudes about interaction (e.g. affability, comfortableness, relaxation, intimacy, nervousness).

Bolton (1979: 47) succinctly describes the attributes of a good listener during verbal lulls as:

> '**Attends to the other.** His posture [listener] demonstrates that he is really there for the other person [storyteller].

> **Observes the other.** He [listener] sees that the speaker's [storyteller's] eyes, facial expressions, posture and gestures are communicating. When you are distracted by the other's words, you may 'hear' his body language more clearly.

> **Thinks about what is communicating.** He ponders [listener] what the other [storyteller] has said. He considers the

variety of responses he might make. Then he selects the one that he thinks will be most facilitative.

Many people who are good listeners achieve this through the power of identification. Many attempts at communicating have resulted in failure due to a lack of exploration of the listener's worldview in terms of what is relevant to them. It is a golden rule for any storyteller that wants to be listened to, to explore the area of interest of the listener.

This is further substantiated by Mackay's (1994: 113) observation that

> many people's favourite subject is themselves. As long as they hear messages about themselves, they will be attentive. As long as the message has some implications for them [listeners] they will listen. As long as the message [story] relates to their own circumstances, they will get involved.

Due to the human psyche man instinctively responds to news of war, murder etc. because he sees the potential relevance to himself and as such listens to the intrigues of the story. From the biblical perspective Jesus made extensive use of parables in His discourses (Matthew 13:3, 10, 13, 34–35, 53; Mark 3:28, 4:2–13). He spoke in ways that were relevant and stimulating by identifying with the needs of the people (area of interest) even on temporal issues.

Relevance is an effective switch in communication that creates involvement and the much-desired symbiotic milieu, as a common ground of interest between the storyteller and listener. This creates a bond of cooperativeness in discourse, which reflects that the listener's feelings and views are important to the storyteller and opens the door for effective communication. The connecting bridge that enhances effective storytelling of the Gospel is to begin with the felt needs of the people.

The principle of suspense

One of the most important principles of storytelling in effective communication is the ability of the storyteller to capture the audience's attention and keep them on the edge of their seats asking what will happen next, while the storyteller delays it as much as possible. One way of achieving this is by the use of prosody to build suspense. Using only his voice, the storyteller can create a feeling of expectation and create an atmosphere of expectation that something exciting is about to happen.

There exist two kinds of suspense, as signalled by the storyteller's prosody, one of which is sudden climax, which is an unexpected dramatic moment in the story, such as a startling revelation or a sudden momentous climax. Such climatic suspense is announced by a steep increase of intensity and pitch on the keyword introducing the climax. Within the time domain of the climax, pitch, intensity and vowel duration are strongly emphasised.

Then there is the increasing climax which is split into two parts, both made up of a clause. The first part builds up the expectation and ends with the key word announcing an action (e.g. 'He opened the jar and then—'), while the second part of the clause gives the actual revelation that takes place ('—there was a sleeping giant'). One primary method of creating suspense is to set up a threat early in a story. For instance in a horror story, suspense ends when the wicked character is defeated, resulting in the removal of the threat; until then the audience must keep asking themselves what terrible thing is going to happen. This was a common feature in Jesus' stories and parables as most of His introductory statements were at times comparisons between two dissimilar features, and so His audience listened with rapt attention as they were held spellbound by the captivating power of His narrations, characters and events of the storyline or parables. For instance in the story of the Good Samaritan, the tapestry of the storyline reveals the use of suspense to illustrate kingdom truth. In fact the genesis of His narration must have arrested His audience as the audience were quite acquainted with the notoriety of bandits, thieves and robbers along the Jerusalem–Jericho route. The famous Jewish historian Josephus affirmed this as he noted that Pompey destroyed a group of brigands while Jerome also spoke about Arab robbers in his time. Naturally with such storycraft, the audience were held spellbound and would have guessed what would befall the Jewish traveller: indeed according to Jesus' narration the man was attacked and wounded 'when he fell into the hands of robbers. They stripped him of his clothes, beat him and went away, leaving him half dead' (Luke 10:30). But Jesus further heightened the suspense by the introduction of the story characters of the Levite, the priest and the Samaritan. The audience would have been kept guessing what the aftermath of the encounter of the characters with the wounded man would be, but the first two characters that ought to have shown compassion and assisted the Jewish man were more preoccupied with their piety rather acts of mercy. Through the power of irony Jesus further put the listeners on the edge of their seats as the third character was introduced in the storyline: the character who actually brought about the resolution of the story as the age-old prejudice and rivalry of the Jews were shattered and the concept of neighbourhood was translated for the audience.

The principle of heart preparation

The effectiveness of a preacher in communication of the Gospel through storytelling does not revolve around head knowledge but the preparedness of the heart of the preacher. Richard Cecil noted that a sermon that has more of 'head infused into it than heart will not be borne home with efficacy to the hearers' (cited in Bounds online). The pulpit of most preachers is almost bereft of the supernatural due to imbalance in their orientation in sermon preparation and delivery. Many often focus on head knowledge without the instrumentality of prayer. Such preachers may at best inform and educate the listeners but will not transform them as Paul asserted in his first letter to the church in Corinth, Chapter two verse four according to International Standard Version (ISV) that: 'my message and my preaching were not accompanied by clever wise words but by the display of the spirit's power'. The man of faith that raised over a million pounds in the 19th century in England through the power of prayer and faith in God, George Muller, distinguished between head knowledge and instrumentality of prayer and their effects in ministry as he stated that, 'Learned commentaries I have found to store the head with many notions and often also with the truth of God but when the Spirit teaches through the instrumentality of prayer and meditation, the heart is affected. The former kind of knowledge generally puffs up, and is often renounced when commentary gives a different opinion and also is found good for nothing when it is to be carried out in practice.' Prayer is the art of wrestling with heaven for an earthly manifestation of our hearts' desires. Prayer is an invitation from a finite being to the infinite being to get involved in his endeavour. It is when our knee is on the ground that our heart and spirit are deeply focused on the mercy seat of God. Prayer is a true force, generating energy and sustaining us. This was quite visible in the lives of the apostles as the Early Church was created at the place of prayer and sustained by her ability to rend the heavens (Acts 4:24, 31–33, 5:14). A man who desires divine endorsement on his pulpit ministry must know how to make a deal with heaven – his knees, body and voice are not strangers to the host of heaven. He must be an abiding supplicant who recognises that the earth will yield its increase only if heaven opens up. These words paint a graphic picture of the need for every preacher to be a man of prayer. One of the greatest secrets of the success of the ministry of Jesus was not rooted in storytelling alone but in the preparation of His heart that empowered Him to communicate effectively. Jesus began His ministry with prayers (Luke 3:21, 22) and likewise every preacher irrespective of the homiletical style must consistently seek divine enablement to bring about the desired effect on the listener. Jesus prayed at the commencement of His ministry but He must certainly have prayed for strength and anointing of the Holy Spirit. If Jesus needed the anointing of the Holy Spirit before He ministered to people, how much more any preacher? Many are engaged in head knowledge development to the detriment of their spiritual empowerment. Robert Murray McCheyne's earnest cry is a vivid illustration of futility of head preparation as he noted 'in the morning I was more engaged in preparing the head more than the heart. This has frequently been my error, and I have always felt the evil of it especially in prayer. Reform it then, O Lord! Enlarge my heart and I shall preach' (cited in Bounds online).

During many times in Jesus' ministry, Jesus withdrew from the crowd and the disciples to pray alone. He often went up on a mountain side or went to solitary places to pray. Sometimes He even went to pray before dawn (Matthew 14:23; Mark 1:35, 6:46; Luke 5:16). Though fellowship with the brethren is quite important, consistent intense moments of prayer are indispensable to an effective public ministry. It is in such undisturbed quietness (Psalm 23:2) that our souls will be ready for sweet communion with God. One of my favourite children's Sunday School songs captures the uniqueness of prayer: it says 'Prayer is the key, Prayer is the key, Prayer is the master key, Jesus started with prayer and ended with prayer, Jesus is the master key.' It is worthy of note in that there is a distinctive emphasis on prayer being the key. The emphasis is as instructive as the noun 'key', which is a metaphor for unlocking the door which literarlly contains valuables, implying that prayer is the access route to the treasures of heaven. The indispensability of prayers to man is noted in the second stanza of the song, as 'Jesus started with prayers and ended with prayers' implies that Christ has provided an effective model for the Church.

The effectiveness of the saints of the Early Church must have been the by-product of the adoption of Jesus' model of success [prayers] as the men and women of the Early Church were saints who made heaven visible on earth with the demonstration of the Power of God. They encountered so much persecution, tribulations and challenges but they were men and women who had visited heaven with their voices and were well acquainted with the one who controls the affairs of all men (Acts 2:42). The scripture captures the heroic exploits of these men of prayers (Acts 2:47, 4:4, 5:15, 6:4.)

The reason why the Elishas of our generation are asking the question of Elisha of old, 'Where is the Lord God of Elijah?' is probably to do with poor communion with the God of Elijah, as many preachers are caught in the web of being busy preaching, counselling, attending meetings and carrying out social actions but forget to maintain the greatest influence on their ministries by disconnecting from their moments of communion with God. Elijah was undeniably a man subject to like passions as most preachers are but the scripture according to James (5:16b) noted he prayed. It seems this is definitely a distinction between most men and Elisha, as some preachers are best described as comedians who make use of storytelling, but their stories only entertain rather than challenge, confront and transform the listeners as the Holy Spirit works in their heart. Many teach and talk about prayer but do little of praying but 'men ought to pray and not faint'.

Charles Spurgeon (cited in Adegboye 2007: 189) adds, 'Prayer is the slender nerve that moveth the muscles of omnipotence.' How marvelous is the sight of a man who enjoys the splendor of conversations with the divine, such can not but be a blessing to others.'

E.M. Bounds said,

> Each leader must be pre-eminently a man of prayer. His heart must graduate in the school of prayer. No learning can make up for the failure to pray. No earnestness, no diligence, no study, no gifts will supply its lack. Talking to men of God is a great thing, but talking to God for men is a greater still. He will never talk well and with real success to

men for God who has not learned well how to talk to God for men. More than this, prayer less words are deadening words.

The basis of an effective ministry is birth at the secret place of prayer. When approached by the people about secret of his success George Whitefield said, 'For days and weeks at a time I am on my face before God in vocal or silent prayers unto God.' This is a form of persistence in prayer as Jesus commands us in Mathew 7:8. The Amplified Bible makes this very clear; 'Keep on seeking and you will find; keep on knocking [reverently] and the door will be opened to you. For everyone who keeps on seeking finds and to him who keeps on knocking, the door will be opened.'

The spirituality of a preacher should be patterned after Jesus Christ, as He is our source. The functionality of a preacher is only in relationship and union with Christ for there lies the provision for power for the spiritual life. Christ is our role model and our leader and as such we are instructed in the New Testament to be imitators of Christ. One of the greatest vehicles for divine enablement for preachers is Holiness; Holiness is the precursor for the anointing of the Holy Spirit. The writer of the book of Hebrews (1:9) stated that 'for thou loveth righteousness and hatest iniquity, the Lord thy God shall anoint thee with oil of gladness above thy fellows'. In the context of the above passage, the exaltation of Jesus Christ was attributable to a life of righteousness which is further asserted in the Gospel according to John (14:30) as he noted, 'the prince of this world cometh and found nothing in me'. Unblemished character is much more convincing in presence evangelism than any proclamation. The whole essence of storytelling the Gospel is not to create amusement among the listeners but to bring about an inner transformation leading to an outward manifestation in conformity with biblical standards in the life of the listener. A sinful life with very good head knowledge will but best achieve nothing, as sin insulates grace. The hand of a man that has experienced

God's grace and power turns into disgrace at the door of sin. Apostle Paul in Romans chapter 6:1 asked the Church in Rome a rhetorical question, 'How can we continue in sin and ask grace to abound? God forbid'. A preacher that lives a sinful life and uses storytelling in communicating the Gospel will at best be remembered as an entertainer and not a preacher by the listener as the inherent power of the Gospel that should bring about transformation to the listeners from such a preacher has been insulated by sin.

Chapter 6

Conclusion

'Stories are the creative conversion of life itself into a more powerful, clearer, more meaningful experience. They are the currency of human contact.'
Robert McKee

The power of storytelling as a tool for effective communication cannot be over-emphasised. Storytellers make use of metaphor, images and symbols, which creates connectedness with the listener. Stories were passed down the generations through oral tradition centuries ago.

There has been a rapid change in communicative style as a result of cultural shifts. Steffen (1994: 92) noted this within the American context:

> Beginning in the 1960s, a movement towards nature began among the Youth of America that influenced communicative style preferences to move towards the concrete and transcendence. With the advent of MTV, the shift became complete for a large majority. The verbal, concrete, short term, multi-sensory experience replaced the visual print media with its focus on a logical, sequential format. We live in a day where communication is dominated by television. It is a post literate age. We are now on oral, musical and visual culture. The use of narrative story is primary.

Due to the global cultural shift which has had ripple effects on virtually every sphere of our existence, it is a common phenomenon that the most popular TV programmes in the Western world are 'reality' shows, talk shows, entertainment shows and soap operas. For instance in Britain you have *The Jeremy Kyle Show* on ITV1, *Big Brother*, *Trisha*, *Emmerdale* and *Coronation Street* while the American scene is dominated by shows like *Jerry Springer, Survivor, The Osbournes, American Pop Idol, The Oprah Winfrey Show* and *Larry King Show* to mention just a few.

There is no denying the dominant influence the media has on people today, especially young people who spend an incredible amount of time watching television or using computers. In the *Word for Today* of 14th January 2007, a daily devotional by Bob Gass, he noted that it is estimated that young people aged 14–24 see over 4,000 violent images during these years. Steffen (1994: 92) noted that 'Television (and videos) through dramatized life narrations connects well with a growing number of baby boomers, baby busters and ethnics.'

Today's media have tremendous influence on people: some TV programmes serve 'menus' that nourish hedonism and amorality, thereby blurring the line between an acceptable moral code in most communities and expressions of personal values. This is further compounded by the trivialisation of traditional family values by the mass media as promiscuity, lewdness and co-habitation are creating a warped orientation on marriage and its sacredness. The American Academy of Paediatrics (AAP) advised that children should watch TV for only two hours but observed that American children watch TV for four hours daily. The impact of TV programming has been identified by the AAP as they recommend that children under two years should be excluded from having TV, computers or video games at all due to the critical developmental stage as this might constitute a diversionary avenue for children experiencing holistic development through exploration and social skills. Obviously television can be an educational avenue, and as such there must be a conscious balance between leisure and educational opportunities for the holistic development of children.

The dominant role that the media plays in shaping character is underscored by Sweet (2000: 86). In comparison with modernity in relation to the emerging cultural trend termed postmodernity, he noted that:

> Postmodern culture is image-driven. The modern world was word-based. Its theologians tried to create an intellectual faith, placing reason and order at the heart of religion. Mystery and metaphor were banished as too fuzzy, too mystical, and too illogical. After forfeiting to the media the role of storyteller, the Church now enters a world where story and metaphor are at the heart of spirituality.

Images are visual metaphors and in an image-driven culture we will need to rediscover the use of metaphor and narrative to elicit a response to the story of Jesus. Contemporary preachers must realise that these media images or products are carefully selected and packaged to have the maximum effect on individuals in society. Serious preparation and ideologies normally accompany the production and delivery of these images and items.

The contemporary preacher is then faced with the challenge of communicating effectively with the baby boomers and Gen-Xers who are not receptive to boring linear communication but respond very well to narrative methods. John Walsh (2003: 116) agrees that 'most people born after the Baby Boomers, receive information best in the form of stories'. As they are not linear thinkers but relational thinkers, 'they want information and they want it straight. But they want it in a way that holds their interest. Stories are the best way to reach to this new breed of thinker.' This is summed up by Calvin Miller (cited in Johnston 2001: 64) who says that, 'The more you know about your audience, the greater your chances of achieving your persuasive goals.'

Leslie Newbigin (1991: 152) observes that the inability of the Church to understand the mindset of its target audience can lead to failure:

By failing to understand and take seriously the world in which it is set, so that the gospel is not heard but remains incomprehensible because the Church has sought security in its past instead of risking its life in a deep involvement with the world. It can fail by allowing the world to dictate the issues and the terms of the meeting. The result then is that, the world is not challenged at its depth but rather absorbs and domesticates the gospel and uses it to secularise itself.

The paradigm shift of the worldview necessitates that the Church must equally respond to meet the challenges of effectively reaching the un-churched. Lesley Newbigin (1991: 12) subscribes to this approach, when he affirms that: 'I am trying to talk about the Gospel – good news about something which happened and which, in that sense, does not change. The way of telling it, understanding it, however does change.'

Postmoderns are no longer content with intellectual philosophy but are now open to spiritual experiences, unlike the modern dispensation where logical and systematic arguments were the bedrock of the era which failed to provide sufficient answers to humanity's innermost needs which led people to experiment in spirituality.

Since Gen-Xers are not likely to be won over by rational apologetics of preachers then preachers need to adopt storytelling by learning to understand the stories of prevailing culture and using such stories to reach today's generation with the truth.

Preachers now, more than ever before, need to emulate Jesus' model of storytelling. As Steffen (1996: 125) observed, Jesus 'never wrote a book on systematic theology, yet he taught theology wherever he went. He often used parabolic stories to teach audiences to reflect on new ways of thinking about life.' Storytelling in preaching brings about the character of the Gospel as a living story. As Ryken (1979: 35) observes, 'the Bible is more than any other single thing, a book of stories. If you doubt this, imagine yourself trying to describe the content of the Bible to someone who has never heard of the Bible. You would very quickly find yourself describing what happens in the Bible and tell what happens to tell a story.' Storytelling in preaching re-enacts the story nature of the Bible to the twenty-first century audience, whose worldview has been shaped by their pluralistic communities.

The act of storytelling the Word is a bridge-building exercise by a preacher to connect the biblical worldview to the contemporary listener; as Steffen (1996: 123) observed, 'approximately seventy-five percent of the Bible is cast in a narrative genre, it becomes obvious that God is a storyteller.' The narrative approach of storytelling is a jewel of inestimable worth to a preacher as it is a natural tool for effective communication of the good news. Storytelling as a natural tool utilised by Jesus Christ, is quite foundational to the Christian faith and as such with a good understanding of the Christian stories is pivotal to the faith of the adherents.

Storytelling the Word creates a community of storytellers as this creates connectedness birthing friendship evangelism as Steffen (1996: 124) observes: 'people find it easy to repeat a good story. Whether the story centres on juicy gossip or the gospel of Jesus Christ, something within each of us wants to hear and tell more stories.' Stories are a great evangelism tool in the hands of a preacher or the laity.

> The Gospel is never an idea! The gospel is an event through which God enters our lives in Jesus Christ. We tell stories in order that people can participate in this gospel reality ... We let stories work because in reality we are seeking to make the gospel happen in human lives. This is a very different goal from one that seeks to explain the gospel. When we explain, we usually begin with more of the idea and then give an illustration to help people grasp the idea. This is metaphor as illustration. I am convinced that metaphors of illustrations do not serve the living gospel of our Lord Jesus as metaphors of participation. We ought to seek to tell stories through which realities of the text become realities of the hearer.' (Jensen 1993: 111, 113)

Storytelling in preaching has tremendous impact as it allows the preacher to construct a desired identity and delve into the culture of the listener as stories connect our imaginations and emotions. Storytelling effectiveness is not limited to preaching but has a broad-spectrum role at all levels of Christian education as it is an alternative approach to communicate with non-linear thinkers. McKinney (1984: 317) made a strong case for storytelling to educators in the West that they 'should not try to make all of the world's peoples into linear thinkers. They will encourage global thinkers to communicate through stories, proverbs, poetry and epoch drama. They will insist that they learn to preach homo[i]letical sermons.' This clarion call by McKinney to educators almost two decades ago is more relevant today than when he made his observation; as the worldview of those in the pulpit is almost being shaped by the worldview of the world. This creates a dynamic tension that calls for ingenuity on the part of a preacher to be exercised and this is attainable by adopting the age-old practice of storytelling to those that are in and outside the pew in order to communicate the Gospel effectively.

The use of storytelling in preaching is not only educational but creates connectedness with human emotions and imagination. The heinous crime of murder and adultery committed by David (2 Samuel 11) seemed to have been neatly concealed until David had a personal transformation as the power of imagination of Nathan (through the vivid use of metaphors that rang in the ears and heart of David) brought him to his knees before God (as the story created action and involvement in Nathan's narration). The magnitude of his repentance cannot but be appreciated as he expresses his anguish for his misdeeds in Psalm 51. Bausch (1984: 16, 27) agrees as he posits that 'Systematic theology engages the intellect, storytelling engages the heart and indeed the whole person.'

In the light of the foregoing, it is imperative to note that storytelling provides an effective approach to communicate the Gospel in the light of the changing worldview. Stories are quite effective to communicate with the growing population of relational thinkers. The ability of stories to connect with human emotion and imagination makes them a tremendous tool in the hands of a preacher to communicate the good news. The art and science of storytelling has biblical precedent, as Christ endorsed it and provides a great opportunity to preachers to preach and teach cross-culturally.

The need for preachers to be realistic in view of the changes in the cultural climate is quite obvious, while still staying true to the Word by not removing the ancient landmarks of the Gospel. There exists the need for preachers to contextualise the Gospel in order to communicate effectively with the twenty-first century listener as change and institutional values cannot be negotiated.

Leonard Sweet opines that there exists a dynamic relationship that a preacher must maintain in the communication of the Gospel in relation to change, methodology and the sacredness of the good news to the listeners as changes in worldview necessitate contextualisation while the preacher does not change the sacredness of the good news. He notes, 'Both continuity and change are essential to an institution' and he further asserts that, 'The gospel is like "living water" ... water fills any receptacle without retaining the form of any. The container doesn't matter. Content stays the same, containers change.' And he insists that in terms of sharing the Gospel, first-century imperatives demand twenty-first-century containers in order to be effective.

Effective communication through storytelling is predicated on the interplay of dynamic principles in a story, which includes the openness and participativeness of the listener as this elicits the listener's involvement and contribution to the story. Connectedness is the ability of the storyteller to take the audience on a fantastic journey of discovery through the use of nonverbal nuances, words and their imagination as irrelevant details are eliminated to create a climate of effective communication.

The principle of unity, coherence and emphasis creates sequence with the structure of a story, which rests on the crest of a well-woven storyline that is unified, devoid of loose threads and a smooth transition from one plot to another. The only recipe for unity in a storyline is to just keep it simple as much as possible. Each word and sentence must lead the listener towards a greater understanding of the overall theme.

Storytelling is an effective tool for communication as long as the storyteller utilises the interplay of principles ranging from point of focus, suspense which makes the audience look forward to the final resolution of the story and the plot which is the scaffolding upon which the story's characterisation is built. The principle of listening places enormous responsibility on the storyteller to comprehend the verbal and non-verbal nuances of the listener.

Reflection and Application

1. Can you identify the various social and cultural values in your domain that have gradually been eroded as a result of the shift in the prevailing culture and how these have negatively and positively influenced the communication of the Gospel?
2. Can you identity with reasons responsible for the fluidity of culture in the last fifty years and why the Church seems to be off tangent in the communication of the Gospel?
3. A well-told story will not only rekindle divine truth in the minds of the listener but is equally instructional as it connects with human emotion and allows the listener to live out grace from the story.
4. As a believer, how would you communicate the Gospel to an audience who have a different worldview from the Christian worldview? Do you think storytelling the Gospel can make a difference?
5. The understanding of the cultural trend can be utilised as a point of engagement in communicating the Gospel in the West. Have you ever thought of using plots in movies to introduce your subject to your listener?

Bibliography

Books

Abram, David, 1997, *The Spell of the Sensuous: Perception and Language in a More-Than-Human World*, New York, Pantheon Books.

Adedibu, Babatunde, 2007, *Impact of Postmodernity on Second Generation Nigerians in Churches in South East London*, MA Thesis University of Wales, Unpublished.

Adegboye, George, 2007, *Men of Like Passion*, UK, Sophos Books.

Allen, D., 1989, *Christian Belief in a Postmodern World: The Full Wealth of Conviction*, Westminster, John Knox Press.

Anderson, Walter Truett, 1995, *The Truth About the Truth: De-Confusing and Re-Constructing the Postmodern World*, New York, G.P. Putman's Sons.

Bailey, Jeff, 1998, 'Association of Vineyard Churches USA Board Report: Perspectives on Church, Gospel and Culture in the 21st Century', unpublished document.

Banks, I., 1997, *A Song of Stone*, United Kingdom, Abacus Books.

Bausch, William, 1984, *Storytelling Imagination and Faith*, Connecticut, Twenty-third Publications.

Bausch, William, 1996, *Storytelling the Word*, Connecticut, Twenty-third Publications.

Bolton, Robert, 1979, *People Skills – How to Assert Yourself and Resolve Conflicts*, New York, Simon and Schuster.

Bosch, D., 1991, *Transforming Mission*. Maryknoll Orbis.

Bounds, E.M., *Power Through Prayer*: www.biblebelievers.com/em_bounds/index.html

Buechner, Friedrick, 1982, *The Sacred Journey*, New York, Harper and Row.

Clark, Evelyn, 2004, *Around The Corporate Campfire*, Tennessee, Insight Publishing Company.

Connor, Steven, 1989, Postmodernist Culture: An Introduction to Theories of the Contemporary, Oxford, Blackwell Publishers.

Dake, Finis Jennings, 1995, *The Dake Annotated Reference Bible* (Kings James Version), Georgia, Dakes Sales Inc.

Daniel-Rops, Henri, 1962, *Daily Life in the Time of Jesus*, New York, Hawthorn Books.

De Mello, Anthony, SJ, 1986, *One Minute Wisdom*, New York, Doubleday.

Dodd, C.H., 1937, *The Apostolic Preaching and Its Developments, Three Lectures*, Chicago, Willett, Clark and Company.

Dodd, C.H., 1961, *Parables of the Kingdom*, New York, Scribner's.

Dorcy, Mary Hean, OP, 1983, *Saint Dominic's Family*, Rockford, IL: TAN Books.

Douglas *et al* (eds), 1980, *Illustrated Bible Dictionary*, Leicester, Inter Varsity Press.

Drane, John, 2001, *The McDonaldization of the Church*, Macon, Smith and Helwys Publishing.

Driscoll, M., 2004, *The Radical Reformission: Reaching Out Without Selling Out*, Grand Rapids, Zondervan.

Duck, Steve, 1992, *Human Relationships*, London, Sage Publishers.

DuPree, Max, 1989, *Leadership is an Art*, Melbourne, Australia, Australian Business Library.

Farrar, Steve, 1995, *Finishing Strong*, Oregon, Multnomah Publishers.

Flory, Richard W. and Miller, Donald E. 2000, *GenX Religion*, New York, Routledge.

Fonck, Leopold, 1998, *The Parables of Christ*, Harrison, Roman Catholic Books.

Forgas, J. and Williams, K. (eds), 2001, *Social Influence: Direct and Indirect Processes*, Philadelphia, Psychology Press.

Gibbs, E. and Coffey, I., 2000, *Church Next: Quantum Changes in Christian Ministry*, Leicester, Inter-Varsity Press.

Green, Colin and Robinson, Martin (2008), *Metavista: Bible, Church and Mission in an Age of Imagination*, Milton Keynes, Authentic Media.

Grenz, S. 1996, *A Primer on Postmodernism*, Grand Rapids, Eerdmans.

Griffith, Joseph, 2000, *Speaker's Library of Business Stories, Anecdotes and Humor*, New York, Prentice Hall.

Harvey, D., 1990, *The Condition of Postmodernity*, Blackwell, London.

Haughton, Rosemary, 1973, *Tales From Eternity: The World of Faerie and the Spiritual Search*, London, George Allan & Unwin.

Hillborn, David, 1997, *Picking up the Pieces – Can Evangelicals Adapt to Modern Culture?*, London, Hodder and Stoughton.

Hutchcraft, R., 2000, 'The battle for a generation', in McDowell, S. and Wiley, R. (eds), *Josh McDowell's Youth Ministry Handbook – Making the Connection*, Word.

Jensen, Richard A., 1993, *Thinking in Story: Preaching in a Post Literate Age*, Lima, OH: C. S. S. Publishing.

Johnston, Graham, 2002, *Preaching to a Postmodern World: A Guide to Reaching Twenty-first Century Listeners*, Leicester, Inter-Varsity Press.

Josephus, V., *Jewish Antiquities Book 1–3*, translated by H. St. J. Thackeray, Boston, Harvard University Press.

Kimball, Dan, 2003, *The Emerging Church – Vintage Christianity for New Generations*, Grand Rapids, Zondervan.

Lewis, C.S., 1982, 'Sometines Fairy Stories May Say Best Whats to be Said', in *On Stories and Other Essays or Literature*, Harvest Books.

Lewis, R. and Lewis, G., 1983, *Inductive Preaching: Helping People Listen*, Westchester, Crossway.

Litherland, Janet, 1991, *Storytelling from the Bible: Make Scripture Live for All Ages Through the Art of Storytelling*, Chicago, Meriwether Publishing.

Mackay, Hugh, 1994, *Why Don't People Listen?*, Australia, Pan Macmillan Publishers.

McFague, Sallie, 1982, *Metaphorical Theology*, Philadelphia, Fortress Press.

McGrath, A., 1994, *Bridge Building: Communicating Christianity Effectively*, Leicester, Inter-Varsity Press.

Meyer, F.B., 1983, *Great Men of the Bible*, Vol. 2, Grand Rapids, Zondervan.

Miles, S., 2000, *Youth Lifestyles in a Changing World*, Buckingham, Open University Press.

Murray, S, 2004, *Post-Christendom: Church and Mission in a strange new world*, Paternoster, London.

Nash, Robert N., Jr, 1997, *An 8 Track Church in a CD World: The Modern Church in a Postmodern World*, Macon, GA, Smyth & Hewlys.

Newbigin, Leslie, 1989, *The Gospel in a Pluralist Society*, Grand Rapids, Eerdmans.

Newbigin, Leslie, 1991, *Truth to Tell: The Gospel As Public Truth*, Grand Rapids, Eerdmans.

Newbigin, Leslie, 1995, *The Open Secret: An Introduction to the Theology of Mission*, London, SPCK.

Niebuhr, H.R. 1951, *Christ and Culture*, New York, Harper and Row.

Pellowski, Anne, 1990, *The World of Storytelling*, New York, H.W. Wilson Co.

Philips, W.G. and Brown, W.E., 1991, *Making Sense of Your World*, Chicago, Moody Press.

Polsky, Howard W. Wozner, Yaella, 1989, *Everyday Miracles; 1989, The Healing Wisdom of Hasidic Stories*, Northvale, NJ, Aronson.

Quicke, J. Michael, 2003, *360 Degree Preaching*, Grand Rapids, Michigan, *Baker Academic*.

Robinson, Haddon W., 2001, *Biblical Preaching: The Development and Delivery of Expository Messages*, Grand Rapids, Baker Academic.

Roxburgh, Alan, 2005, *The Sky is Falling*, Eagle, Idaho, ACI Publishing.

Seilhamer, Frank, n.d., cited at: www.yfcasiapacific.org/pdf /evangelismbk1.pdf.

Shea, John, 1980, *Stories of Faith*, Chicago, Thomas More Press.

Sire, J.W. 1997, *The Universe Next Door: a Basic World-view*, Downers Grove, Inter-Varsity Press.

Smith, Colin, 2002 'Keeping Christ Central in Preaching', in Carson, D.A. (ed.) *Telling the Truth: Evangelizing Postmoderns*, Grand Rapids, Zondervan.

Steffen, Tom, 1996, *Reconnecting God's Story to Ministry: Cross Cultural Storytelling at Home and Abroad*, La Habra, CA: Center for Organisational and Ministry Development.

Sweet, Leonard, 2000, *Post-Modern Pilgrims: First Century Passion for the 21st Century World*, Nashville, Broadman and Holman.

Tomlinson, D., 1995, *The Post-evangelical*, London, Triangle.

Veith Jr, GE 1995, *Postmodern times: a Christian guide to contemporary thought and culture*, Crossway Books, Wheaton.

Walker, Alan, 1957, *The Whole Gospel for the Whole World*, New York, Nashville, Abingdon Press.

Walsh, B.J. and Middleton, J.R., 1984, *The Transforming Vision*, Downers Grove, Inter-Varsity Press.

Walsh, John, 2003, *The Art of Storytelling: Easy Steps to Presenting an Unforgettable Story*, Chicago, Moody.

Ward, Graham, 2000, *Cities of God*, New York, Routledge.

Waznak, Robert, 1983, *Sunday after Sunday: Preaching the Homily as Story*, Mahwah, NJ, Paulist Press.

White, Ellen G., 1941, *Christ's Object Lessons*, Washington DC: Review & Herald.

White, William R., 1982, *Speaking in Stories*, Minneapolis, Augsburg Publishing.

Wilson, Paul Scott, 1995, A *Concise History of Preaching*, Nashville, TN, Abingdon.

Journals and Papers

Cray, Graham, 2000, 'Postmodernity Under Construction', *The Gospel and Our Culture Newsletter*, Issue 27: www.gospel-culture.org.uk.

Dobson, A.E., 1993, 'When the foundations tremble: a conversation with Leith Anderson, Ed Dobson, Os Guinness, and Haddon Robinson', *Leadership*, vol. 14, no. 2.

Mckinney, Lois, 1984, 'Contextualizing instruction: contributions to missions from the field of education' *Missiology*, 12 (3): 311–26.

Ryken, Leland, 1979, 'The Bible, God's Storybook', *Christianity Today*, October 5:34–38.

Shaw, Gordon, *et al.*, 1998, 'Strategic Stories: How 3M is rewriting business planning', *Harvard Business Review*, Boston, Harvard Business School Press.

Sine, T., 2003, 'Globalisation, creation of global culture of consumption and the impact on the Church and its mission', *Evangelical Review of Theology*, vol. 27, no. 4: 353–70.

Steffen, Tom, 1997, 'Reaching Resistant, People Through Intentional Narrative', Paper presented at the Evangelical Missiological Society, South West Regional Meeting, April 4.

Steffen, Tom, 1994 'A narrative approach to communicating the Bible, part 2', *Christian Education Journal* 24(3): 86–97.

Topel, John, 'On Being "Parabled"', *The Bible Today*, December 1976.

Newspapers

Darren Behar, *Daily Mail*, 17th October 2003.

Index

Printed in the United Kingdom by
Lightning Source UK Ltd., Milton Keynes
141136UK00001B/39/P